The Life of Galileo

Published to coincide with the first production at the National's
Olivier Theatre, this translation by Howard Brenton of one of
Brecht's masterpieces brings to the play the vigour and incisiveness
of Brenton's own work for the theatre while remaining entirely
faithful to Brecht's remarkable original.

'The new translation by Howard Brenton is muscular and slangily
eloquent . . .'
  Irving Wardle, *The Times*

'Mr Brenton's version is mostly excellent. Its clarity is in line with
the best aspects of the play . . .'
  Robert Cushman, *Observer*

Bertolt Brecht

THE LIFE OF GALILEO

Translated by Howard Brenton

METHUEN · LONDON

First published in Great Britain in 1980 by Eyre Methuen Ltd.
11 New Fetter Lane, London EC4P 4EE, by arrangement with
Suhrkamp Verlag, Frankfurt am Main

Reprinted 1980
Reprinted with revisions 1981
Reprinted 1982 by Methuen London Ltd

Translation copyright © 1980 by Stefan S. Brecht

Original work entitled *Leben des Galilei*
Copyright 1940 by Arvid Englind Teaterforlag, a.b.,
renewed June 1967 by Stefan S. Brecht
Copyright © 1955 by Suhrkamp Verlag, Frankfurt am Main

All rights reserved

Set IBM by ⳅ Tek-Art, Croydon, Surrey
Printed in Great Britain by
Richard Clay (The Chaucer Press) Ltd,
Bungay, Suffolk.

ISBN 0 413 47140 3

Translator's Note
Translating this play has cheered me up. That angry but circumspect, tough but sly attitude which Gramsci called 'Pessimism of the intellect: optimism of the will' shines in its text. Its optimism is certainly not sentimental about reason's chances nor, indeed, about humanity's —

> THE LITTLE MONK: But won't the truth, if it is the
> truth, prevail — with us or without us?
> GALILEO: No. No no. As much of the truth will prevail that
> we make prevail.

And the intellect's pessimism says — this play is about truth betrayed. As the cold war in 1980 grips minds and distorts reality more fiercely than ever, that betrayal three hundred and fifty years ago is still with us. We have probably yet to live its full consequences under the mushroom clouds and the 'rain of fire'.

And the will's optimism says — yes, but. Yes the play is about truth betrayed, but not quite. Not quite because a student of Galileo's, a boy in the first scene a man in the last, smuggles a book across a border to us, in the future. As in the play, so in life. The blood runs cold with fear when one thinks of the courage men and women find to carry truth over borders in our day. 'Unhappy the land that needs heroes.'

One warning, if warning it be to you. There is a lot of loose talk about Brecht's 'Humanism', his 'Ambiguity'. Brecht was a humanist, for marxism is, to a marxist, the true humanism. Brecht was, like anyone with a sense of humour, a dab hand at irony and saying two or more things at once — 'Ambiguity'. But he was a communist. Oh yes, like it or not, he was a communist and a communist writer. Milton said he wrote *Paradise Lost* to 'Justify the ways of God to men'. Brecht, like a godless Milton of the twentieth century, one foxy eye on the great theme of the stars above the other on the human mess below, set out to justify the ways of communism to men and women. The new science of Galileo's time is, in a mighty double meaning at the heart of the play, marxism now. I don't think it too far-fetched to see *The Life of Galileo* as Socialist Literature's *Paradise Lost*.

It is a desperately timely play.

H.B.

Characters

Galileo Galilei
Andrea Sarti
Signora Sarti, *Galileo's housekeeper and Andrea's mother*
Ludovico Marsili, *a rich young man*
Signor Priuli, *the Bursar of the University of Padua*
Sagredo, *Galileo's friend*
Virginia, *Galileo's daughter*
Federzoni, *a lens grinder, Galileo's collaborator*
The Doge
Senators
Cosimo de' Medici, *Grand Duke of Florence*
Court Chamberlain
Older Lady in Waiting
Younger Lady in Waiting
Grand Duke's Lackey
Two Nuns
Two Soldiers
Woman
Old Woman
Fat Prelate
Two Scholars
Two Monks
Two Astronomers
Very Thin Monk
Very Old Cardinal
Father Christopher Clavius, *an astronomer*
Little Monk

Cardinal Inquisitor

Cardinal Barberini, *later Pope Urban VIII*

Cardinal Bellarmin

Two Ecclesiastical Secretaries

Two Young Ladies

Filippo Mucius, *a scholar*

Signor Gaffone, *Rector of the University of Pisa*

Ballad Singer

Ballad Singer's Wife

Vanni, *an iron-founder*

Official

High Official

Individual,

Monk, peasant, frontier guard, clerk, men, women, children

Written 1938-39 and 1945-47. Collaborator: M. Steffin.
Music: Hanns Eisler. First produced in the Zurich Schauspielhaus,
9 September 1943, by Leonard Steckel, scenery by Teo Otto, with
Steckel as Galileo.

This translation first produced in the Olivier auditorium of the
National Theatre, London, on 13th August 1980, directed by
John Dexter, designed by Jocelyn Herbert, with Michael Gambon
as Galileo.

GALILEO GALILEI, TEACHER OF MATHEMATICS
AT PADUA, DECIDES TO PROVE THE NEW COPERNICAN SYSTEM

> In the year sixteen hundred and nine
> The light of knowledge began to shine
> In Padua city in a little house
> Galileo Galilei sets out to prove
> The sun is still but the earth is on the move

Galileo's humble Study in Padua

It is morning. A boy, Andrea, the son of the housekeeper, brings on a glass of milk and a bread roll.

GALILEO, *washing the upper part of his body, snorting and cheerful:* Put the milk on the table. Don't touch my books.

ANDREA: Mother says we've got to pay the milkman. If we don't he'll run circles round the house screaming.

GALILEO: Describe. You describe a circle, Andrea.

ANDREA: He'll describe circles round the house, screaming.

GALILEO: And the bailiff will come straight at us — making what kind of line between two points?

ANDREA: The shortest.

GALILEO: Right. Present for you. Behind the star charts.

Andrea fishes out a large wooden model of the Ptolemaic system from behind the star charts.

ANDREA: What is it?

GALILEO: An astralabe. It shows the way the ancient astronomers said the stars go round the earth.

ANDREA: How?

GALILEO: We will investigate. Begin at the beginning. Description.

ANDREA: There's a little stone. In the middle.

GALILEO: The earth.

ANDREA: There are layers, all round the stone. One over the other. Like globes.

GALILEO: How many?

ANDREA: Eight.

GALILEO: They are the crystal spheres.

ANDREA: There are balls, stuck to the globes.

GALILEO: The planets.

ANDREA: They've got strips of wood, with words painted on.

GALILEO: What words?

ANDREA: Names of stars.

GALILEO: Such as?

ANDREA: The moon's the lowest. And above the moon there's the sun.

GALILEO: Now. Make the sun move.

ANDREA, *moving the globes*: That's great!, But we're all shut in.

GALILEO, *drying himself*: That's what I felt, first time I saw the thing. A lot of us do feel it. *He throws Andrea the towel for him to rub his back dry.* Walls, globes, immobility! For two thousand years men believed the sun, the planets and all the stars revolved around them. The Pope, cardinals, princes, captains, merchants, fishwives and school boys thought they were stuck dead still, at the centre of that crystal ball. But now we're flying headlong out into space, Andrea. The old age is dead, a new age is born. For the last hundred years men have held their breath, expecting something. The cities and men's minds are packed with rubbish — superstition and plague. But now we can say — because that's how it is, that's not how it's going to stay. For now we know — everything moves! I like to think it began with the ships. For as long as men could remember, the ships crawled by the coasts, in sight of land. But suddenly they shot out, over the seas. The continents laugh — for the word is out in our old Europe, an amazing rumour — there are new continents. And because our ships sail to them, the vast, dreaded ocean is suddenly — just a pond. And so a desire is fanned to find the cause of all things, how a stone falls when you drop it, how it rises when you throw it. Everyday there's a new discovery. The old and deaf get the young to yell in their ears news of the latest sensation. When I was a young man in Sienna, I saw two building workers use a five minute argument to replace a thousand year old method of moving granite blocks, by a new and more rational tackle. There and then I knew – the old age is dead, a new age is born. Soon mankind will know the truth about his home, the heavenly body on which he lives. The answers in the old books won't do anymore. Where belief sat, now sits doubt. The whole world says – that's what the old books say. Now let's look for ourselves. The most solemn truth gets tapped on the shoulder. All that was never doubted, we doubt. So a wind of questions lifts the gold embroidered robes of princes and prelates to show – just fat or thin legs, legs like our legs. The wind turns into a gale of laughter. But the waters of the earth drive our new machines. And in the rope and sail shops five hundred hands move in the harmony of a new scheme of things.

I predict that in our lifetime astronomy will be talked of in the streets. Even the sons of fishwives will run to school. The people of our cities cry out for the new ideas. It will delight them that a new astronomy says – 'Now the earth moves too.' Always we were told –'The stars are fixed to a roof of crystal to stop them falling down.' But now we've got the courage to set them free and flying through space – like we send our ships, flying through oceans. And the earth rolls happily round the sun and the fishwives, merchants, princes, and cardinals and even the Pope roll with it. Overnight the universe lost its centre and this morning – they are countless. Each and none at all is the centre. Suddenly there's a lot of room. The ships go far on the sea, the stars go far into space – even in chess, nowadays, the rooks have taken to flying all over the board.

What does the poet say? 'Oh early morning of beginning' –

ANDREA:

'Oh early morning of beginning
Oh scent of winds from new shores.'

You'd better drink your milk up. People'll be round here again to see you.

GALILEO: Did you understand what I told you yesterday?

ANDREA: What? That Kippernicus and his revolving?

GALILEO: That.

ANDREA: No. What do you want me to understand that stuff for? It's very difficult. I'm only eleven in October.

GALILEO: But that's why I want you to understand. You above

all. I work so hard and buy pricey books and don't pay the milkman — so that someone like you can understand.

ANDREA: But in the evening I see the sun's not where it was in the morning! It's not standing still. Not! Not!

GALILEO: See? What do you see? You see nothing. You just gawk. Gawking's not seeing. *He sets the iron wash-stand in the middle of the room.* That's the sun. Sit down. *Andrea sits on the chair. Galileo stands behind him.* Where is the sun — on your right or on your left?

ANDREA: Left.

GALILEO: And how does it get over to your right?

ANDREA: Carry it, of course.

GALILEO: Is that the only way? *He picks him up together with the chair and rotates him through a semicircle.* Where's the sun now?

ANDREA: Right.

GALILEO: Has it moved?

ANDREA: No.

GALILEO: What has moved?

ANDREA: Me.

GALILEO, *bellows*: Wrong! Stupid idiot! Not you, the chair!

ANDREA: But I went with it!

GALILEO: Exactly. The chair is the earth. You're sitting on it.

SARTI, *she has come in to make the bed. She has been watching*: What is it you're up to with my son, Signor Galilei?

GALILEO: I'm teaching him to see, Signora Sarti.

SARTI: By dragging him round the room?

ANDREA: Don't, Mum. You don't understand.

SARTI. But you do, eh? A young gentleman wants lessons. Fashionable clothes and a letter of recommendation. *She hands it over.* Andrea will say two times two is five next. He muddles up everything you tell him. Yesterday he proved to me the earth goes round the sun. He's got it into his little head a man called Kippernicus worked it out.

ANDREA: He did! Didn't he, Signor Galilei? Tell her.

SARTI: You really do fill him up with that rubbish? He'll go

yelling it all round the school. Then the ecclesiastical
gentlemen will be down on my neck. You ought to be ashamed
of yourself, Signor Galilei.

GALILEO, *breakfasting*: As a result of our investigations and
after bitter controversy between us, Andrea and I have made
discoveries we can no longer keep from the world. A great era
has dawned, Signora Sarti. A new age, in which it's a joy to
be alive.

SARTI: Indeed. And will milk get paid for in this new age?
Pointing to the letter of recommendation. Help me out and
don't send this one packing too. It's the milk bill I have to
investigate. *Exit.*

GALILEO, *laughing*: Let me swallow this lot anyway! *To
Andrea*: So we did get something into your head yesterday!

ANDREA: I just told her that to shock her. But it's not true. All
you did was turn the chair round sideways. Not over – like
that. *He makes a sweeping movement with his arm.* Because
I'd fall off. That's why.

GALILEO: But I did prove it to you –

ANDREA: But I worked it out last night. If the earth turns I'll
hang upside down, all night. And that's a fact.

GALILEO, *takes an apple from the table*: Right. That's the earth.

ANDREA: Don't take examples like that, Signor Galilei. You
can prove anything with examples like that.

GALILEO, *putting the apple back*: All right.

ANDREA: Prove anything with examples, if you're sly enough.
I can't drag my Mum round on a chair, like you dragged me.
What's it show anyway, if an apple is the earth? Shows nothing.

GALILEO, *laughing*: You just don't want to know.

ANDREA: All right. Pick it up again. Why don't I hang upside
down all night?

GALILEO: The earth. You standing on it. *He sticks a splinter
from a firelog into the apple.* Now the earth rotates.

ANDREA: And now I'm hanging upside down.

GALILEO: Look! Look hard! Where is your head?

ANDREA, *points at the apple*: There. Upside down.

GALILEO: What? *He turns the apple back.* Isn't your head where
it always is? Look. Don't your feet stay on the ground? Because

the earth turns, do you stand on your head? *He takes the splinter out and turns it upside down.*

ANDREA: No. Why don't I notice the earth turning, then?

GALILEO: Because you go with it! You, the air, everything on the earth.

ANDREA: And why does the sun look as if it moves?

GALILEO, *turning the apple with the splinter again*: Right. At your feet you see the earth. You go with it, so you don't see it move. But look up. There's the lamp, above your head. Now I turn you. What's above your head now?

ANDREA, *follows the turn*: The stove.

GALILEO: And where's the lamp?

ANDREA: Down below.

GALILEO: Aha!

ANDREA: Great. That'll shock her.

Ludovico Marsili, a rich young man, comes in.

GALILEO: This place is like a pigeon loft.

LUDOVICO: Good morning, Sir. My name is Ludovico Marsili.

GALILEO, *studying his letter of recommendation*: You've been in Holland?

LUDOVICO: Where I heard a great deal about you, Signor Galilei.

GALILEO: Your family owns estates in the Campagna?

LUDOVICO: It's my mother. She wants me to see the world. Sniff around and see what's going on.

GALILEO: And in Holland you sniffed that I was going on?

LUDOVICO: Well, my mother wants me to pick up a bit of science.

GALILEO: Private tuition – ten scudi a month.

LUDOVICO: Thank you, Signor.

GALILEO: What are your interests in life?

LUDOVICO: Horses.

GALILEO: Huh huh.

LUDOVICO: I've got no head for science.

GALILEO: Huh huh. Fifteen scudi a month.

LUDOVICO: Thank you, Signor.

GALILEO: It'll have to be early in the morning. Your loss I'm afraid, Andrea. He's paying, you're not.

ANDREA: I'm going. Can I have the apple?

GALILEO: Yes. *Andrea goes out.*

LUDOVICO: I hope you'll bear with me. It's just that science always seems to go against commonsense. Like that odd tube they're selling in Amsterdam. I took one to pieces, really carefully. A case of green leather and two lenses, one like that — *He draws a concave lens in the air.* and one like that — *He draws a convex lens in the air.* They say one makes things big and the other makes things small. Commonsense says they'll cancel each other out. Wrong. You look through it and everything's five times as large. Typical science.

GALILEO: What do you see five times as large?

LUDOVICO: Church spires. Pigeons. Everything in the distance.

GALILEO: You, yourself, saw church spires enlarged five times?

LUDOVICO: Oh yes, Signor.

GALILEO: Two lenses? *He makes a sketch on a piece of paper.* Did it look like that? *Ludovico nods.* How old is the invention?

LUDOVICO: Not more than a few days, when I left Holland. At least it'd not been on the market longer than that.

GALILEO, *almost friendly*: Why study physics? Why not horsebreeding?

Mrs Sarti comes in unnoticed by Galileo.

LUDOVICO: My mother thinks a little science is good for the social graces. All the world sips science with its wine, these days.

GALILEO: Pick a dead language. Or theology. Be easier on the brain. *He sees Signora Sarti.* All right. Tuesday morning. Early.

Ludovico goes out.

GALILEO: And don't give me that look. I took him on.

SARTI: Because I caught your eye, just in time. The University Bursar is coming up.

GALILEO: Bring him in. An absolutely vital man. There could be five hundred scudi in it. Then — no more private pupils.

Signora Sarti brings in the Bursar. Galileo is now fully dressed, scribbling figures on a scrap of paper.

GALILEO: Morning. Lend me half a scudi. *The Bursar fishes a coin out of his purse. Galileo gives it to Signora Sarti.* Sarti, send Andrea round to the spectacle maker. I want two lenses. Here are the specifications.

Signora Sarti goes out with the slip of paper.

BURSAR: I've come to discuss your application for an increase in your salary to 1,000 scudi. Sadly, I cannot recommend it to the University. You know that at the moment the Faculty of Mathematics does not attract a large intake of students. Mathematics is, in a sense, something of a lost art. Not that the Republic does not value, indeed cherish it. It's not as necessary as philosophy, or as practical as theology, but it does give its adherents endless pleasure.

GALILEO, *over his papers:* My dear man, I can't get by on 500 scudi.

BURSAR: But Signor Galilei, you give two, two hour lectures a week. Your extraordinary reputation surely attracts all the private pupils you need. Do you not give private lessons?

GALILEO: Too many! I teach and teach – but when can I learn? God Almighty, I'm not an all knowing clairvoyant, like the gentlemen of the Faculty of Philosophy. I'm stupid. I know absolutely nothing. I'm forced to patch up the holes in the little I do understand. But when? When am I meant to research? Sir, my science is greedy for knowledge. We have no answers to the most basic questions, only hypotheses. But we demand proofs. How can I work on them, when just to keep a roof over my head I'm forced to hammer into the nearest thick, concrete brained skull with the cash the fact that parallel lines meet at infinity?

BURSAR: Signor Galilei. Do not utterly forget that though the Republic does not pay you as much as some princes would, it does guarantee you freedom in your research. We in Padua let protestants into our lectures, we even give them degrees! When it was proved, proved Signor Galilei, that Signor Cremoni made blasphemous statements what did we do? Not only did we not hand him over to the Inquisition, we bumped up his salary. Even as far away as Holland they know – Venice is the Republic where the Inquisition is powerless. That is of some, small worth to you, an astronomer – working in a science with a history of scant respect for the teachings of Holy Church!

GALILEO: You handed Signor Giordano Bruno over to Rome. Why? He taught the theories of Copernicus.

BURSAR: Not because he taught the theories of Copernicus, which are blatant nonsense anyway, but because he was not a Venetian. Nor did he hold a University post. So don't bolster up your argument with the charred remains of a man burnt at the stake. And it's not clever to shout a name like that, on which the church has laid an anathema. Not here, not even here. For all our freedom.

GALILEO: For you, freedom is good business — no? You publicise how everywhere but here the Inquisition rules and burns. So you get good teachers on the cheap. You cash in on freedom from the Inquisition by paying lousy salaries.

BURSAR: That is outrageously unjust! What good would it do you if you had all the time in the world, but a pig ignorant monk of the Inquisition could suppress your every thought? No rose without a thorn, no princes without monks, Signor Galilei.

GALILEO: And what good is all the freedom in the world to research, with no time to do it? What happens to the results? All right. Kindly show the gentlemen of the Signoria these Investigations Into the Laws of Falling Bodies. *He points to a bundle of manuscripts.* Ask them if they're worth a few more scudi.

BURSAR: Infinitely more, Signor Galilei.

GALILEO: Not infinitely more. 500 more.

BURSAR: What is worth scudi, brings scudi. If you want money, produce something saleable. Knowledge is a market. You can only sell your work for what the buyer can sell it for. For example, the philosophy Signor Colombe sells in Florence brings the Prince in at least 10,000 scudi a year. Your Laws of Falling Bodies made a stir, yes. They applaud you in Paris and Prague. But the gentlemen applauding you there sadly do not pay the University of Padua what you cost it. Your problem is your subject, Signor Galilei.

GALILEO: Ah, I understand. Free research plus free trade equals fat free profits.

BURSAR: A facile remark. I don't understand your cynicism. The flourishing trade of the Republic is hardly an object of contempt. Nor can I, Bursar of a great University for many years, be so flippant about scientific research. *While Galileo gives longing glances towards his work table.* Consider the world outside! The slavery beneath which the sciences groan —

a whip cut from the leather bindings of old books! There you do not ask why a stone falls, you ask what Aristotle wrote on it. Eyes are only for reading. What's the use of a new law of falling bodies, if the only law needed is for bodies cringing flat on the ground in fear? Set against that the endless delight of our Republic in your ideas, however outlandish they may be! Here you can work! Here you can research! No one spies on you, no one oppresses you! Our merchants know what better linen means in the trade war with Florence, so they know what you mean when you call for better physics — better looms. Don't the demands of industry advance physics? Think why great men follow your research, visit you, have your discoveries demonstrated to them — men for whom time is money. So do not despise trade, Signor Galilei. No one here will tolerate your work being disrupted, or you being harassed by outsiders. You can work here. Admit it.

GALILEO, *despairing*: Yes.

BURSAR: As for making ends meet, invent something charming. Elegant. Like your splendid proportional compasses, with which you need no mathematics at all to — *He counts on his fingers.* protract lines, calculate compound interest on capital, reproduce ground plans of buildings on a large or small scale and determine the weight of cannonballs.

GALILEO: A toy.

BURSAR: A scientific instrument that astounded and delighted eminent men — and sold well? No toy, a miracle. I hear even General Stefano Gritti can find square roots with it.

GALILEO: A miracle indeed. But Priuli, you give me an idea. Maybe I've got just the thing. *He picks up the sheet of paper with the sketch on it.*

BURSAR: You have? It would be the solution. *He stands.* Signor Galilei, we know you are a great man. A great but angry man, if I may say so.

GALILEO: Yes, I am angry. THAT is what you'd pay me for, if you weren't stupid! For I'm angry with myself. But you do all you can to make me end up angry with you. I admit I find it fun to muck in with you gentlemen of Venice, in your famous arsenal, your shipyards, your gun foundaries. But you leave me no time to think through, to expand, to develop the scientific ideas that burst into my mind when I work there. You muzzle the ox that threshes. I am 46 years old. Nothing I have done gives me peace.

BURSAR: Then I will disturb you no longer.

GALILEO: Many thanks.

The Bursar goes out. Galileo remains alone for a few moments and begins to work. Then Andrea comes running in.

GALILEO, *working*: Not eaten the apple?

ANDREA: I want it to show mother she's revolving.

GALILEO: Andrea. I must say something to you. Don't talk to people about our ideas.

ANDREA: Why not?

GALILEO: The authorities have forbidden them.

ANDREA: But they're true.

GALILEO: But they're forbidden. And for we physicists, there's another reason. You and I can't prove what we know to be true. Even the teachings of the great Copernicus are not proved. They are only hypotheses. Give me the lenses.

ANDREA: Half a scudi wasn't enough. I had to leave my coat.

GALILEO: What will you do in the winter with no coat?

A pause. Galileo arranges the lenses on the sheet of paper that bears the sketch.

ANDREA: What's a hypothesis?

GALILEO: When you think something is likely, but have no facts. Look at Signora Felice, down there by the baker's. She's got a child at her breast. She gives milk to the child, the child doesn't give milk to her. That is a hypothesis, right up to when you go down and see and prove it. But faced with the stars we are like worms with clouded eyes. We can hardly see at all. The old teachings, believed for a thousand years, are caving in. There is less wood in those gigantic structures than in the props that are meant to shore them up – the many old laws, which explain little. Whereas the new hypothesis has few laws, which explain a lot.

ANDREA: But you proved everything to me.

GALILEO: No. I only showed you what could be true. Understand? A hypothesis. A very fine one, nothing contradicts it.

ANDREA: I want to be a physicist too, Signor Galilei.

GALILEO: I don't blame you. Seeing the vast number of questions to be cleared up in our field. *He has gone over to the window and looked through the lenses. He is moderately interested.* Take a look, Andrea.

ANDREA: Holy Mary. Everything comes close. The bell on the campanile's quite clear. I can read the copper letters – Gratia Dei.

GALILEO: That'll rake us in 500 scudi.

2

GALILEO PRESENTS A NEW INVENTION TO THE REPUBLIC OF VENICE

Virtues of the great are crude
Galileo likes his food
Please don't be shocked and try to cope
With the truth about the telescope

The Great Arsenal of Venice, by the Harbour

Senators, at their head The Doge. To one side, Galileo's friend Sagredo and the fifteen year-old Virginia Galilei. She carries a velvet cushion on which lies a telescope about 60 centimetres long and in a crimson leather case. Galileo on a dais. Behind him the stand for the telescope, attended by the lens grinder Federzoni.

GALILEO: Your Excellency. Noble Signoria. As a teacher at your University of Padua and a director of your great arsenal here in Padua, I see my duty as not only to fulfil my high responsibility of teaching but also to benefit the Republic with practical inventions. Therefore, humbly and with great pleasure, I present and demonstrate to you today a completely new instrument – my long distance glass or telescope, manufactured in your world famous arsenal, according to the highest scientific and christian principles – the fruit of seventeen years painstaking research.

Galileo leaves the dais and stations himself next to Sagredo. Clapping. Galileo bows.

GALILEO, *aside to Sagredo, softly*: Waste of time.

SAGREDO: You can pay the milkman now.

GALILEO: Oh yes, it'll make them money. *He bows again.*

BURSAR, *he steps out onto the dais*: Your Excellency. Noble
   Signoria. Once again, a page of glory in the great book of the
   arts is resplendent with the name of Venice. *Polite applause.*
   A scientist of world wide reputation presents to you, and you
   alone, a highly marketable tube, for you to manufacture and
   sell as you choose. *Stronger applause.* And have you thought
   how in time of war we can now, with this tube, tell the
   strength and composition of an enemy's fleet a full two hours
   before he can ours, giving us decisive tactical advantages? *Very
   strong applause.* And now your Excellency, noble Signoria,
   Signor Galilei asks you to accept this instrument of his genius,
   this flower of his talent, from the hand of his charming daughter.

*Music. Virginia comes forward, curtsies and presents the telescope
to the Bursar, who presents it to Federzoni. Federzoni places it
on the stand and adjusts it. The Doge and the Senators climb
the dais and look through the telescope.*

GALILEO, *aside to Sagredo*: I don't know if I'm going to get
   through this charade. They just think they've got a money-
   spinner on their hands. But last night I pointed that tube at
   the moon.

SAGREDO: What did you see?

GALILEO: It has no light of its own.

SAGREDO: What?

SENATOR: I can see the fortifications of Santa Rosita, Signor
   Galilei! And they're having lunch in that boat. Grilled fish.
   My mouth's watering.

GALILEO: Why did astronomy stand still for a thousand years?
   It had no telescope.

SENATOR: Signor Galilei.

SAGREDO: They're talking to you.

SENATOR: You see too much with this thing. I'll have to tell
   the women in my house – no more bathing on the roof.

GALILEO: Do you know what the Milky Way is?

SAGREDO: No.

GALILEO: I do.

SENATOR: One could ask at least ten scudi for a thing like
   this, Signor Galilei.

Galileo bows.

VIRGINIA, *brings Ludovico to her father*: Ludovico wants to congratulate you, Father.

LUDOVICO, *embarrassed*: I congratulate you, Sir.

GALILEO: I improved it.

LUDOVICO: Yes Sir. You made the case red. In Holland it was green.

GALILEO, *turns to Sagredo*: I begin to wonder. Can I prove a certain theory with this thing?

SAGREDO: Galileo —

BURSAR: Your 500 scudi are found, Signor Galilei.

GALILEO, *ignoring him*: Of course I'm wary of any premature conclusion.

The Doge, a fat, unassuming man, has approached Galileo and is trying with clumsy dignity to speak to him.

BURSAR: Signor Galilei, his Excellency The Doge.

GALILEI: Of course! The 500! Are you satisfied, your Excellency?

DOGE: Unfortunately, in the Republic we always need an excuse to enable our City Fathers to remunerate our scholars.

BURSAR: On the other hand, where would the incentive be, eh Galilei?

DOGE, *smiling*: We need the excuse.

The Doge and the Bursar lead Galileo to the Senators, who surround him. Virginia and Ludovico walk slowly away.

VIRGINIA: Did I do it all right?

LUDOVICO: I think it was all right.

VIRGINIA: What's got into you, then?

LUDOVICO: Oh, nothing. Perhaps a green case would have been just as good.

VIRGINIA: I think they're all very pleased with father.

LUDOVICO: And I think I'm beginning to learn something about science.

10TH JANUARY 1610: WITH THE TELESCOPE GALILEO MAKES
DISCOVERIES IN THE SKY WHICH PROVE THE COPERNICAN
SYSTEM. WARNED BY HIS FRIEND OF THE POSSIBLE
CONSEQUENCES OF HIS RESEARCH, GALILEO ASSERTS HIS
FAITH IN REASON.

> January the tenth sixteen hundred and ten
> Galileo finds out God's heaven is not there

Galileo's Study in Padua

*Night. Galileo and Sagredo, wrapped in thick cloaks, at the
telescope.*

SAGREDO, *looking through the telescope, in an undertone*: The
edge of the crescent is uneven, jagged and rough. On the dark
half, near the edge of light, there are luminous spots. They
come into existence, one after another. Light fans out from
the spots, wider and wider, until it merges with the bright half.

GALILEO: How do you explain the luminous spots?

SAGREDO: No. It can't be.

GALILEO: It can. Mountains.

SAGREDO: On a star?

GALILEO: Gigantic mountains, their peaks gilded with the rising
sun, while night still covers the lower slopes. You see the light
descending from the highest peaks into the valleys.

SAGREDO: But that destroys all the astronomy of the last
thousand years.

GALILEO: But that's how it is. Except for myself, no man has
ever seen what you see now. You are the second.

SAGREDO: But the moon can't be another earth, with mountains
and valleys. Anymore than the earth can be a star.

GALILEO: The moon *can* be an earth, with mountains and
valleys, the earth *can* be a star. An ordinary heavenly body,
one among thousands. Look again. Is the dark half of the
moon completely dark?

SAGREDO: No. When I look hard, it has a faint, ashen light.

GALILEO: What light?

SAGREDO: ?

GALILEO: It is light from the earth.

SAGREDO: Nonsense. How can the earth shine, a dead body with mountains, forests and seas?

GALILEO: The same way the moon shines. Because earth and moon are lit by the sun. What the moon is to us, we are to the moon. Now it sees us as a crescent, now half full, now not at all.

SAGREDO: So there is no difference between moon and earth?

GALILEO: Evidently not.

SAGREDO: Less than ten years ago a man was burnt in Rome. Giordano Bruno. He said that.

GALILEO: He did. Now we see it's true. Keep your eye at the telescope, Sagredo. You are looking at a new truth — there is no difference between heaven and earth. Today is the tenth of January, 1610. Man writes in his diary — Heaven abolished.

SAGREDO: That is appalling.

GALILEO: I've discovered another thing. Perhaps even more astounding.

The Bursar rushes in.

BURSAR: Forgive the late hour. Please — we must talk privately.

GALILEO: Signor Sagredo can hear what I hear, Signor Priuli,

BURSAR: You may not find it congenial if the gentleman hears what has happened. It is absolutely incredible.

GALILEO: Signor Sagredo's used to hearing the absolutely incredible when he's with me.

BURSAR: Far too true, I fear. *He points at the telescope.* Look at it! That marvel, that miracle! And now throw it away. It's worth nothing, absolutely nothing.

SAGREDO, *who has been walking around uneasily*: Why?

BURSAR: Are you aware that what you called the fruit of seventeen years painstaking research, you can buy on every street corner in Italy? And — the final insult — stamped made in Holland? While I'm talking a dutch freighter is unloading 500 telescopes in our harbour!

GALILEO: Oh?

BURSAR: Your calm baffles me.

SAGREDO: Why worry? I tell you, in the last few days Signor Galilei has made revolutionary discoveries about the universe with that instrument.

GALILEO, *laughing*: Take a peep.

BURSAR: This disaster's discovery enough for me. I'm the fool who got his salary doubled — for that trash. It's only a fluke the gentlemen of the Signoria, thinking they'd bought exclusive commercial rights, didn't look down the thing and see it being sold off on a corner for the price of a sandwich — and by any street trader, seven times enlarged.

Galileo guffaws with laughter.

SAGREDO: My dear Signor Priuli. I know nothing of this instrument's commercial significance, but its worth to philosophy is beyond comprehension —

BURSAR: Philosophy? Signor Galilei's a mathematician. What's he got to do with philosophy? Signor Galilei. You designed the city an excellent water pump. Your irrigation system is reliable. Cloth weavers praise your loom. How could I expect this chicanery from you?

GALILEI: Hold on Priuli. Sea voyages are still long, dangerous and costly, no? Sailors need a signpost. A clock in the sky? I believe certain stars have completely regular motions. With the telescope they will be clearly seen. New star charts can save millions of scudi in the navigation of ships of trade —

BURSAR: Don't go on! You've trodden all over me enough. I gave you sympathy and you made me look a clown before the whole city. I'll go down as the University Bursar who lost his head over a worthless telescope. You can laugh — you got 500 scudi out of it. But I tell you, I am an honest man and the world disgusts me.

He goes out slamming the door behind him.

GALILEO: I almost like him when he's angry. You got that? A world where you can't do business disgusts him!

SAGREDO: Did you know about the dutch telescope?

GALILEO: Yes, of course. But I made our miserly officialdom one twice as good. How can I work with a bailiff leaning over my table? And Virginia will have to be fixed up with a dowry soon. She's not bright. And I like books, not only on physics, books about everything, and I like my food. I get my best ideas over a good feed. A rotten age! They don't pay me what they pay a coachman who delivers their wine casks. Four bundles of firewood for two lectures on mathematics. All right I've squeezed 500 scudi out of them, but some of the debts are twenty years old. Give me five free years of research and I'll prove everything! Something else to show you.

SAGREDO, *hesitates to take the telescope*: I feel a kind of fear, Galileo.

GALILEO: You are going to look at one of the shining, milk white clouds of the Milky Way. Tell me. What is it?

SAGREDO: Stars. Innumerable stars.

GALILEO: In the constellation of Orion alone there are five hundred. They are the distant and countless other worlds the burnt man spoke of. He didn't see them – his intuition told him they were there.

SAGREDO: But even if the earth is a star, we're a long way from Copernicus's assertion that the earth goes round the sun. The moon may revolve around the earth – but no other body in the heavens has another revolve around it.

GALILEO: Sagredo, I've been wondering. Two days, I've been wondering. There is Jupiter. Near to Jupiter there are four small stars. I saw them on Monday, but didn't note their position. Today, they've moved again. What's this? I saw four. *Agitated.* Look!

SAGREDO: I see three.

GALILEO: Where is the fourth? We must calculate what movements they make. Here are the tables.

They set to work excitedly. It grows dark on the stage but Jupiter and its satellites remain visible on the curve of the horizon. When it gets light again they are still sitting there, with their winter cloaks on.

GALILEO: Proved. The fourth can only have gone behind Jupiter, where it cannot be seen. There – a star around which another revolves.

SAGREDO: But the crystal sphere to which Jupiter is fixed –

GALILEO: Yes. Where is it? How can Jupiter be fixed to a crystal sphere, if other stars circle around it? No fixed frame in heaven! No still centre in the universe! There is another sun!

SAGREDO: Calm down. You go too fast.

GALILEO: Too fast? Wake up! You're seeing what no man has ever seen! They were right!

SAGREDO: Who? The Copernicans?

GALILEO: They and the burnt man! The whole world was against them – and they were right. Andrea's got to see this. *He runs to the door beside himself and calls out.* Signora Sarti! Signora Sarti!

SAGREDO: Galileo, you've got to calm down!

GALILEO: Sagredo, you've got to get worked up! Signora Sarti!

SAGREDO, *turns the telescope away*: Will you stop running about like a madman?

GALILEO: Will you stop being a dead cod on the slab? The truth has been found.

SAGREDO: I'm not being a dead cod on the slab. It's that if that is the truth, I tremble.

GALILEO: What?

SAGREDO: Have you gone insane? Can't you see what you're tangling with if what you see is true? And you go and shout in the streets – that the earth is a star and not the centre of the universe?

GALILEO: Shout that the whole, vast cosmos of millions of stars does not turn round our tiny earth! Shout that anyone can work it out!

SAGREDO: Work out there are only stars in heaven? And where is God?

GALILEO: What do you mean?

SAGREDO: God. Where is God?

GALILEO, *angrily*: Not there! No more than he's on earth – and if beings came down from the stars to look for him here.

SAGREDO: Where is God then?

GALILEO: I'm no theologian. I'm a mathematician.

SAGREDO: First, you're a man. And I ask you, where is God in your universe?

GALILEO: Within us – or nowhere!

SAGREDO, *shouting*: As the burnt heretic Giordana Bruno said?

GALILEO: As the burnt man said!

SAGREDO: Burnt for saying it!

GALILEO: Because he had no proof. Only intuition.

SAGREDO: I thought you were a realist, Galileo. Seventeen years in Padua, three years in Pisa you placidly taught the Ptolemaic system, as blessed by the Church and confirmed by the scriptures. All the time you thought it a lie, along with Copernicus. But you taught it.

GALILEO: Because I could prove nothing.

SAGREDO, *incredulous*: You really think that makes a difference?

GALILEO: All the difference in the world! Look Sagredo. I believe in man. Which means — I believe in man's reason. Without that belief I'd not have the strength to get out of bed in the morning.

SAGREDO: I tell you, I have no belief in reason. My forty years alive have taught me, again and again, that men are not moved by reason. Show them the red tail of a comet, stir up dark fears in them, and they'll trample each other to pieces. But give them one simple truth, prove it with seven lucid reasons — and they'll laugh in your face.

GALILEO: Rubbish. A slander. I don't understand you. How can you believe that and love science? Only the dead are unmoved by reason!

SAGREDO: How can you confuse man's squalid cunning with reason?

GALILEO: I'm not speaking of their cunning. I know they call a donkey a horse when they sell it, and a horse a donkey when they want to buy it. That's man's cunning. My hope is with the old woman who gives her mule an extra bundle of hay the night before a journey, the sailor who calculates for days lost by storms and lays in provisions, the schoolboy who pops his cap on, when it's proved to him it will rain. My hope is with them because they test reason in everyday life. Yes, I believe in the gentle power of reason over men. No man can see me — *He drops a stone on the floor.* — drop a stone on the floor and say — it does not fall. No man's capable of that! Proof is a sweet seduction. Most of us succumb in the end. Thinking is one of the great pleasures of the human race.

SARTI, *enters*: Do you want something, Signor Galilei?

GALILEO, *who is back at his telescope making notes and very amiable*: Yes, I want Andrea.

SARTI: Andrea's tucked up in bed, fast asleep.

GALILEO: Wake him up.

SARTI: What do you want him for?

GALILEO: I want to show him something that will delight him, something no one's seen since the world began.

SARTI: Not something through your tube again.

GALILEO: Something through my tube again.

SARTI: Drag him out of bed in the middle of the night, for that? You gone mad? That boy needs his sleep. I won't dream of waking him.

GALILEO: Your last word?

SARTI: My last word.

GALILEO: Then, Signora Sarti, you help me. You see a question's come up and we can't agree. Probably our brains are addled by reading too many books. The question is about the heavens, about the stars. Do large things revolve around small things, or do small things revolve around large ones?

SARTI, *mistrustfully*: You never know with you. That a real question, or another bad joke?

GALILEO: A real question.

SARTI: Then I'll give you a quick answer. Do I put the food in front of you, or do you put the food in front of me?

GALILEO: You put it in front of me. Burnt, yesterday.

SARTI: And why was it burnt? Because right in the middle of me cooking it, you yelled for your shoes. Did I get you your shoes?

GALILEO: I suppose − yes.

SARTI: And why did I get you your shoes? Because you do the studying and can pay. So I go round you.

GALILEO: Yes. Yes. Problem solved. Good morning Signora Sarti.

Signora Sarti goes out, amused.

GALILEO: And people like that can't grasp the truth? They'd gobble it down.

A bell for early mass has begun to ring. Enter Virginia in a cloak, carrying a storm lantern.

VIRGINIA: Good morning, father.

GALILEO: What gets you up so early?

VIRGINIA: I'm going with Signora Sarti to early mass.
Ludovico's coming too. What was the night like, Father?

GALILEO: Clear.

VIRGINIA: Can I look through the telescope?

GALILEO: Why? *Virginia is lost for an answer.* It's not a toy.

VIRGINIA: No, father.

GALILEO: Anyway, the telescope's a failure. You'll hear that
all over the place. They sell it in the street for three scudi.
And it's already been invented in Holland.

VIRGINIA: Have you − seen any new things in the sky with it?

GALILEO: Not for you. Just little cloudy spots to the left of
a big star. I've got to get them talked about somehow. *Past his
daughter to Sagredo.* Let's christen them 'The Medici stars',
after the Grand Duke of Florence, eh? *To Virginia*: This will
interest you, Virginia. We're moving to Florence, if we can.
I am writing a letter asking the Grand Duke if he could do with
me as Court Mathematician.

VIRGINIA, *radiant*: At the Court?

SAGREDO: Galileo!

GALILEO: My friend. I need leisure to work. And I want the
fleshpots. With a court position I wouldn't have to hammer
Ptolomy into the heads of private pupils. I'd have time, time,
time, time, time! To work out my proofs. What I have now
is still nothing. A rag bag, bits and pieces. I can't stand up
before the whole world with that. Still there is not one single
proof that any heavenly body circles the sun. But I'll find
proofs, proofs for everyone from Signora Sarti up to the
Pope. My only worry is the court won't take me.

VIRGINIA: Course they'll take you father, with your new stars
and everything.

GALILEO: Go to your mass.

Virginia goes out.

GALILEO: I don't often write letters to the great. *He gives
Sagredo a letter.* Does it have the grand style?

SAGREDO, *reads from the letter*: 'I long for nothing but to be
near you, the rising sun that will flood this age with light.'
The Grand Duke of Florence is nine years old.

GALILEO: He is. You find my letter obsequious? I wonder if

it's obsequious enough. As if I lacked the copper bottomed, genuine humility? If you're qualified in parroting Aristotle you can afford to write a dignified, reticent letter. But the likes of me must go gibbering and crawling to get a decent job. What the hell. I despise people without the brains to fill their bellies.

Signora Sarti and Virginia pass on their way to mass.

SAGREDO: Don't go to Florence.

GALILEO: Why not?

SAGREDO: The monks rule there.

GALILEO: There are great scholars at the Court of Florence.

SAGREDO: Lackeys.

GALILEO: I'll drag them screaming by the ears to the telescope. Even monks are human, Sagredo. Even they can be seduced by reason. Remember, Copernicus demanded they believe his sums − all I demand is they believe their eyes. If truth is too weak to defend itself, it must attack. I'll drag them by the hair, I'll ram their eyeballs up the telescope.

SAGREDO: Galileo, you set out on a fearsome road. It is a night of disaster when a man sees the truth. And an hour of blind stupidity when he comes to believe in men's reason. 'He went into it with his eyes open.' Of whom is that said? Of the man on the road to self-destruction. How can those in power let a man run around free when he knows the truth? Even the truth about the distant stars? Do you think the Pope will hear your truth and say 'Wonderful I'm wrong.' Do you think he'll even listen to you? Go and write in his diary − 'tenth of January, 1610 − Heaven abolished?' How can you walk out of the Republic with the truth in your pocket, waving your telescope in your hand − right into the traps of monks and princes? You're so rational, so sceptical in your science − and so like a wide-eyed little child when it comes to fighting for it in the real world. You don't believe in Aristotle, you do believe in the Grand Duke of Florence! When I saw you just now, at the telescope, looking at your new stars − I saw you standing on burning logs. When I heard you say 'I believe in reason' − I smelt burnt flesh. My friend, I love science. But I love you more. Don't go to Florence, Galileo!

GALILEO: If they want me. I go.

The last page of the letter appears on the curtain.

When I give the new stars I have discovered the illustrious name of Medici, I know that immortality in the starry heavens was glory enough for gods and heroes. But now the illustrious name of Medici gives immortal glory to the stars. I, however, only wish to bring to your notice that I am one of your most loyal and obedient servants, who considers it the highest honour to have been born your subject.

I long for nothing but to be near you, the rising sun that will flood this age with light.

4

GALILEO HAS LEFT THE REPUBLIC OF VENICE FOR THE FLORENTINE COURT. THERE HIS DISCOVERIES WITH THE TELESCOPE MEET WITH DISBELIEF AMONG THE SCHOLARS.

The old way says: do what I do know what I know
The new way says: if you're useless then go

Galileo's House in Florence

Signora Sarti is making preparations in Galileo's study for the reception of guests. Her son Andrea is sitting and clearing away star charts.

SARTI: Ever since we moved to this world-famous Florence, the bowing and scraping and licking of behinds has not stopped. The whole city trudges by this tube — then I have to clean the floor. Not that it does a bit of good. If there was anything in these discoveries, the priests and monks'd be the first to know. Four years I was in the service of Monsignore Filippo and never got a duster round all of his library. Fat leather books right up to the ceiling — and not a love story in sight! And the good Monsignore had two pounds of boils on his bottom from all that sitting over all that science. Now a man like that's got to know what he's doing. And the great viewing today will be another fiasco — and I won't be able to look the milkman in the face, yet again. I said to him, I know how to handle this — plonk a good dinner down in front of the learned gentlemen first, then let them crawl all over the tube. But no. *She mimics Galileo.* 'I've got something else for them.'

A knock below. She looks in the spy mirror at the window.

SARTI: Oh my God, the Grand Duke's here already. And Galileo's still at the University.

She runs down the stairs and lets in the Grand Duke of Tuscany, Cosimo di Medici, with the Court Chamberlain and two ladies in waiting.

COSIMO: I want to see the telescope.

CHAMBERLAIN: Perhaps your Highness will wait patiently until Signor Galilei and the other gentlemen return from the University. *To Sarti:* Signor Galilei has invited the astronomers to verify his new discovery of the Medici stars.

COSIMO: They don't believe in the telescope. They say it's a lot of rubbish. Where have you got it?

SARTI: Upstairs in the study.

The boy nods, points up the stairs and, at a nod from Signora Sarti, runs up them.

CHAMBERLAIN, *a very old man*: Your Highness! *To Signora Sarti:* Must one go up there? I only came because the tutor is ill.

SARTI: The young gentleman will be all right. My boy's up there.

COSIMO, *entering above:* Good evening.

The boys bow ceremoniously to each other. A pause. Then Andrea turns to his work again.

ANDREA, *very like his teacher*: This place is like a pigeon loft.

COSIMO: A lot of visitors?

ANDREA: Stumbling about gawking, understanding nothing.

COSIMO: Is that —

ANDREA: Yes. But hands off!

COSIMO: What's that? *He points at the wooden model of the Ptolemaic system.*

ANDREA: That's the Ptolemaic.

COSIMO: It shows how the sun goes round the earth, doesn't it?

ANDREA: so they say.

COSIMO, *sitting down in a chair, taking the model in his lap:* My tutor's got a cold, so I got out early. It's good here.

ANDREA, *uneasy, he wanders around looking at the strange boy mistrustfully. Finally, unable to resist the temptation any longer, he takes a second model from behind charts, a representation of the Copernican system*: Course — really it's like that.

COSIMO: What's like that?

ANDREA: That's what they say it's like. *He points to his model.* And this is what it's really like.

COSIMO: Oh yes? I wonder why they won't let me see my tutor. The old man was at supper yesterday.

ANDREA: Don't you believe me?

COSIMO: Course I do.

ANDREA: No you don't. *Suddenly pointing at the model in Cosimo's lap.* Give me that back. You don't even understand that one.

COSIMO: You don't need two.

ANDREA: Give it me. It's not a toy for kids.

COSIMO: I'll give it to you, if you learn to be polite.

ANDREA: You're an idiot. Stuff politeness — give it here!

COSIMO: Get off.

ANDREA: I'll teach you how to handle a model. Give it!

COSIMO: Now it's broken. You're pulling my arm off.

ANDREA: We'll see who's right and who's wrong. Say the earth goes round the sun or I'll kick your head in.

COSIMO: Get off! Ginger bastard! You've got to be polite to me.

ANDREA: Ginger bastard am I!

They fight on in silence. Down below Galileo and several professors of the University enter. Behind them Federzoni.

CHAMBERLAIN: Gentlemen. Signor Suri, his Highness's tutor, could not accompany his Highness. A slight chill.

THEOLOGIAN: Nothing serious I hope?

CHAMBERLAIN: No no. Not at all.

GALILEO, *disappointed*: Is his highness not here?

CHAMBERLAIN: His Highness is upstairs. Please do begin, gentlemen. The Court is agog with impatience to know our Great University's opinion of Signor Galilei's extraordinary new instrument and the wonderful new stars.

They go upstairs. The boys are now lying still. They have heard the noise below.

COSIMO: They're here. Let me up. *They stand up quickly.*

GENTLEMEN, *on the way up*: No no, everything's fine — The Faculty of Medicine say there's no question the illness in the Old Town's plague. The miasmas would be killed by this cold weather — Panic's what I fear, not non-existent plague — Just headcolds, typical of the time of year — Not the shadow of a doubt — No no, everything's fine. *Greetings above.*

GALILEO: Your Highness. I am privileged to demonstrate my discoveries to scholars of your University, in your presence.

Cosimo bows formally to all sides, even to Andrea.

THEOLOGIAN, *seeing the broken Ptolomaic system on the floor*: Something's had an accident —

Cosimo bends down quickly and politely hands the model to Andrea. Meanwhile Galileo surreptiously puts the other model away.

GALILEO, *at the telescope*: As your Highness no doubt knows, for some time we astronomers have been in great confusion with our calculations. We use a very old system which agrees with philosophy but not, unfortunately, with the facts. The old system, that of Ptolomy, says the movements of the stars are extremely complicated. An example — the orbit of the Planet Venus is meant to be like this. *He draws on a blackboard the epicyclic orbit of Venus according to Ptolomaic assumptions.* But even if we accept such complex movements, we cannot predict the position of the stars. Stars appear in the skies where they should not. Also, there are star movements for which Ptolomy's system has no explanation. None at all. Such are the movements of four small stars around the planet Jupiter, newly discovered by myself. Gentlemen, I suggest you begin by looking at these satellites of Jupiter, the Medici stars.

ANDREA, *pointing to the stool in front of the telescope*: Please, sit down there.

PHILOSOPHER: Thank you, my child. I fear nothing is that simple, Signor Galilei. Before we apply ourselves to your famous telescope, we beg the pleasure of a disputation. The theme — can such stars exist?

MATHEMATICIAN: A formal disputation.

GALILEO: Why not just look through the telescope and see they exist?

ANDREA: Here, please.

MATHEMATICIAN: Yes, yes. You do, of course, acknowledge that the ancients tell us it is impossible for a star to revolve around any centre but the earth — nor can there be stars which have no support in the heavens?

GALILEO: Yes.

PHILOSOPHER: Leaving aside the possible existence of such stars, of which the mathematician — *He bows to the Mathematician.* — is doubtful, as a philosopher I ask this question — are such stars necessary? Aristotelis divini universum

GALILEO: Can't we speak in the vernacular? My Colleague, Signor Federzoni, doesn't understand Latin.

PHILOSOPHER: Is it important that he understands us?

GALILEO: Yes.

PHILOSOPHER: Forgive me. I thought he was your lens grinder.

ANDREA: Signor Federzoni is a lens grinder and a scholar.

PHILOSOPHER: Thank you my child. If Signor Federzoni insists —

GALILEO: I insist.

PHILOSOPHER: The argument will lose elegance. But it's your house — The cosmos of the divine Aristotle with its mystical, music-making spheres, crystal domes and the gyration of its heavenly bodies and the oblique angle of the sun's orbit and the secrets of the planetary tables and the wealth of stars in the catalogue of the southern hemisphere of the celestial globe is an edifice of such order and beauty, that we would do well to hesitate before disrupting such harmony.

GALILEO: What if your Highness, this minute, looks through the telescope and sees these impossible and unnecessary stars?

MATHEMATICIAN: One might be tempted to reply that if your telescope shows something that cannot exist, it can't be a very reliable telescope, eh?

GALILEO: And what do you mean by that?

MATHEMATICIAN: It would be more productive, Signor Galilei, if you told us the reasons why you claim that, in the highest sphere of the immutable heavens, stars can float about freely in space?

PHILOSOPHER: Reasons, Signor Galilei, reasons!

GALILEO: Reasons? When one glance at the stars demonstrates the truth? This disputation becomes fatuous.

MATHEMATICIAN: At the risk of exciting you further, one might say — what is in your telescope and what is in the heavens, may be two different things.

PHILOSOPHER: It could not be put more tactfully.

FEDERZONI: You think we painted the moons of Jupiter on the lens!

GALILEO: You accuse me of fraud?

PHILOSOPHER: We would never do that. Not in the presence of his Highness —

MATHEMATICIAN: And the telescope, be it your child or your pupil, is made with lavish and undoubted skill —

PHILOSOPHER: And we are utterly convinced, Signor Galilei, that not you or anyone would dare to fix the illustrious name of our ruling house upon stars whose existence was not beyond all possible doubt.

All bow low to the Duke.

COSIMO, *looking round to the ladies in waiting:* Is there something wrong with my stars?

OLDER LADY IN WAITING, *to the Duke*: There's nothing wrong with your stars, your Highness. The gentlemen just wonder if they're really there.

A pause.

YOUNGER LADY IN WAITING: They say you can see the hair on the bear's chest through the telescope.

FEDERZONI: And all sorts of things on the bull.

GALILEO: So gentlemen. Are you going to look or not?

PHILOSOPHER: Of course.

MATHEMATICIAN: Of course.

A pause. Suddenly Andrea turns away and walks stiffly across the room on his way out. His mother catches hold of him.

SARTI: What's up with you?

ANDREA: They're stupid. *He tears himself away and runs off.*

PHILOSOPHER: Deplorable brat.

CHAMBERLAIN: Your Highness. Gentlemen. May I remind you the state ball begins in three quarters of an hour?

MATHEMATICIAN: Why hum and ha about it? Sooner or later

Signor Galilei will have to reconcile his ideas with reality. His moons of Jupiter would break through the crystal sphere.

FEDERZONI: Surprise surprise — there is no sphere.

PHILOSOPHER: Every school book will tell you there is, Sir.

FEDERZONI: Then let's have new school books.

PHILOSOPHER: Your Highness, my respected colleague and I rely on the authority of the Divine Aristotle himself.

GALILEO, *almost obsequious*: Gentlemen. To believe in the authority of Aristotle is one thing — to grasp a fact is another. You say that according to Aristotle there are crystal spheres up there — therefore certain movements cannot take place because the stars would crash through the spheres. But what if you establish these movements as facts? Perhaps that tells you the crystal spheres do not exist? Gentlemen, I beg you, in all humility. Trust your eyes.

MATHEMATICIAN: My dear Galilei. It may seen quaint to you, but I read Aristotle. Then I do trust my eyes.

GALILEO: I'm used to academics — of all disciplines — blinding themselves to the facts, burying their heads as if nothing's changed. I show my observations — they smile. I put the telescope in their hands — and they quote Aristotle. The man had no telescope!

MATHEMATICIAN: Indeed not.

PHILOSOPHER, *sententiously*: If Aristotle is to be dragged through the mud, an authority recognised not only by the ancient sciences but by the Early Fathers of the Holy Church, then the very least one can say is the discussion is superfluous. I avoid the superfluous. And that's that.

GALILEO: Truth is the child of time, not authority. Our ignorance is infinite. Let's shorten it by one cubic centimetre. Why be obsessed with intellectual gymnastics — when now, at last, we can be a little less stupid. I had the incredible good luck to get hold of an instrument and see one, tiny corner of the universe. Not much, but a little more clearly. Let's use that.

PHILOSOPHER: Your Highness, ladies and gentlemen. I wonder where all this may end.

GALILEO: It is not for scientists to ask where the truth will lead.

PHILOSOPHER, *furiously*: Signor Galilei! The truth may lead us absolutely anywhere!

GALILEO: Your Highness. All over Italy tonight, telescopes are pointed at the skies. The moons of Jupiter will not bring down the price of milk. But they have never been seen before — and there they are. So the man in the street thinks — what more can I see, if I open my eyes? You owe him a confirmation! It is not the orbits of a few distant stars that make Italy sit up — it's the news that teachings said to be unshakable begin to totter. Everyone knows there're far too many around anyway. Gentlemen, don't defend teachings that are dying.

FEDERZONI: It's you who ought to be killing them off!

PHILOSOPHER: I would be grateful if your man did not try to offer advice in a scientific disputation.

GALILEO: Your Highness! In the great arsenal of Venice I worked all day with draughtsmen, builders and instrument makers. They taught me many new ways of doing things. Illiterate, they relied on the evidence of their five senses, not worrying where it led them —

PHILOSOPHER: Oho!

GALILEO: Just as our sailors left the coasts, not knowing where they'd reach, or even if they'd survive. If you want to find the true greatness of ancient Greece, that mighty spirit of enquiry, alive today — go to the ship yards.

CHAMBERLAIN: Your Highness, to my dismay this extra-ordinarily instructive conversation runs on a little. His Highness must rest a while before the state ball.

At a sign Cosimo bows to Galileo. The court quickly prepares to go.

SARTI, *places herself in front of the Grand Duke and offers him a pastry*: A cake, your Highness?

GALILEO, *running after them*: But gentlemen. Just look through the thing!

CHAMBERLAIN: His Highness will not neglect to seek the opinion of our greatest living astronomer about your claims. I mean of course Father Christopher Clavius, Chief Astronomer at the Papal College in Rome.

5

UNDAUNTED EVEN BY THE PLAGUE GALILEO
CONTINUES HIS RESEARCH.

a

Galileo's Study in Florence

Early morning. Galileo over his notes at the telescope. Enter Virginia who has a travelling bag.

GALILEO: Virginia! What's happened?

VIRGINIA: The convent's closed. They sent us home at once. There are five cases of plague in Arcetri.

GALILEO, *calls*: Sarti!

SARTI, *enters*: What are you doing home?

VIRGINIA: The plague.

SARTI: Dear God. I'll pack. *She sits down.*

GALILEO: No packing. Get Virginia and Andrea. I'll get my notes.

He runs hurriedly to his table and gathers papers together in great haste. Signora Sarti puts a clock on Andrea, who comes running in, and fetches some bedding and food. Enter a Lackey of the Grand Duke.

LACKEY: His Highness has left the city because of the spreading sickness. He insisted, however, that Signor Galilei be offered the chance to reach safety as well. The coach will be at the door in two minutes.

The Lackey goes out.

SARTI: Get out of the house. Now. Take that.

ANDREA: Why? You don't tell me and I won't go.

SARTI: It's the plague, my child.

VIRGINIA: Wait for father.

GALILEO, *wrapping the telescope in the table cloth:* Put Virginia and Andrea in the coach. I'm just coming.

VIRGINIA: No. We're not going without you. You start packing your books and you'll never come.

SARTI: The coach is here.

GALILEO: Be sensible Virginia. Get in now or the driver will be off. The plague's a serious matter.

VIRGINIA, *protesting as Signora Sarti leads her and Andrea out:* Help him pack the books or he won't come.

SARTI, *from the door:* Signor Galilei! The driver won't wait!

GALILEO: I can't leave, Signora Sarti. Everything's in a mess. I may as well throw away three months of notes if I don't go on one or two more nights. Anyway, the plague's everywhere.

SARTI: You're mad. Come now.

GALILEO: You go with Virginia and Andrea. I'll follow later.

SARTI: They'll close the city in an hour. No one will get out. You've got to come − now!

She goes out. Galileo walks up and down. Signora Sarti returns, very pale, without her bundle.

GALILEO: What are you hanging about for? The coach and the children will go without you.

SARTI: They have. They had to hold Virginia in. They'll look after the children in Bologna. But what about you and cooking your food?

GALILEO: You *are* mad. Stay in a plague city because of cooking? *Picks up his notes.* Don't think me a fool, Sarti. I can't abandon this work. I have powerful enemies and I must prove my theories.

SARTI: No need to apologise. But you are a fool all the same.

b

Outside Galileo's House in Florence

Galileo comes out and looks down the street. Two nuns come past.

GALILEO, *addresses them:* Sisters − can you tell me where I can buy some milk? The milkwoman didn't come today and my housekeeper's out.

ONE NUN: Shops are only open in the Lower Town now.

OTHER NUN: Did you come out of there? *Galileo nods.* They're the houses!

Both nuns cross themselves, murmur an Ave Maria and hurry away. A man comes by.

GALILEO, *addresses him*: Don't you deliver our white bread? *The man nods.* Have you seen my housekeeper? She must have gone out last night. She's not been in the house all day.

The man shakes his head. A window flies open and a woman looks out.

WOMAN, *shouting*: Run! They've got the plague over there!

The man runs away terrified.

GALILEO: Have you seen my housekeeper?

WOMAN: She collapsed. Just down the street. She must have guessed. That's why she got away from you. Selfish cow.

She slams the window shut. Children come down the street. They see Galileo and run away screaming. Galileo turns round. Two soldiers run up, in full armour.

SOLDIERS: Back in your house. Move.

With their long lances they push Galileo back into his house. They bar the door behind him.

GALILEO, *at the window*: Do you know what happened to the woman who collapsed?

SOLDIERS: They take them to the meadows.

WOMAN, *appears at the window again*: All that side of the street is infected. Block it off.

The soldiers rope off the street.

WOMAN: No not like that! Not this side, we're healthy over here! No one can get in our house! No! No! Please – my husband's still in the town. He can't get back to us. You animals! You animals!

She can be heard inside sobbing and screaming. The soldiers go off. At another window an old woman appears.

GALILEO: There must be a fire over there.

OLD WOMAN: They don't bother with fires anymore. Plague's all they think about.

GALILEO: How like them. And like their whole system of government. They just lop us off, like the diseased branch of a fig tree.

OLD WOMAN: You mustn't talk like that. They're helpless.

GALILEO: Are you alone in the house?

OLD WOMAN: Yes. My son sent me a note. He learnt someone opposite died so he didn't come home, thank God. There were eleven cases around here last night.

GALILEO: I blame myself for not sending Signora Sarti away. I have urgent work, but she had no need to stay.

OLD WOMAN: We can't go either, now. Who'd take us in? Don't blame yourself. I saw her. She went out this morning, early. I was taking the bread in. I knew she was ill the way she kept her distance. She probably didn't want to shut your house up. But they find out everything.

A rattling noise is heard.

GALILEO: What's that?

OLD WOMAN: They make a noise to blow away the clouds that carry plague seeds.

Galileo guffaws.

OLD WOMAN: How can you still laugh?

A man comes down the street and finds it blocked off.

GALILEO: Hey you! We're blocked off here and there's no food in the house!

The man has already run away.

GALILEO: You can't let us starve to death here, hey!

OLD WOMAN: Maybe they'll bring something. If they don't I'll put some milk by your door, if you're not afraid. But only after dark.

GALILEO: Hey! They've got to hear us.

Suddenly Andrea stands by the rope. His face is stained with tears.

GALILEO: Andrea! How did you get there?

ANDREA: I was here earlier. I knocked but you didn't open the door. People said —

GALILEO: Didn't you go in the coach?

ANDREA: Yes. But I jumped out on the way. Virginia went on. Can't I come in?

OLD WOMAN: No you cannot. You go to the Ursulines. Perhaps your mother's there.

ANDREA: I've been. They wouldn't let me see her, because she is so ill.

GALILEO: Did you walk all the way? It's three days since you left.

ANDREA: That's how long it took me. Don't be angry. They caught me once.

GALILEO, *helpless*: Don't cry anymore. Listen. I've discovered all kinds of new things. Shall I tell you? *Andrea nods, sobbing.* Remember I showed you the planet Venus? Don't listen to that noise, it's nothing. Venus! Do you know what I've seen? It's like the moon! I've seen it full and I've seen it as a crescent. What do you think of that? I can show you why with a little ball and a light. It proves that planet doesn't have its own light either. And it revolves around the sun, in a simple circle. Isn't that wonderful?

ANDREA, *sobbing*: Course. And it's a fact.

GALILEO, *softly*: I didn't keep her here.

Andrea is silent.

GALILEO: But if I hadn't stayed, it wouldn't have happened.

ANDREA: Will they have to believe you now?

GALILEO: The proofs are complete. Know what? When all this is over here, I'll go to Rome. Then we'll show them.

Down the street come two men, muffled up, with long poles and buckets. On the poles they pass bread through the window to Galileo and then to the Old woman.

OLD WOMAN: There's a woman with three children over there. Leave food there too.

GALILEO: But I've got nothing to drink. There's no water in the house.

Both shrug their shoulders.

Will you come round tomorrow?

ONE MAN, *in a choked voice because of the cloth over his mouth*: Who knows what will come round tomorrow?

GALILEO: If you do, could you pass me up a small book I need, for my work?

THE MAN, *laughs hollowly*: No book matters now. Be glad if you get bread.

GALILEO: That boy's my pupil. He'll get it from the school for you. *The men have already passed on.* It's the map with the period of rotation of Mercury, Andrea.

ANDREA: I'll get it, Signor Galilei. *He goes out.*

Galileo goes back inside. The old woman comes out of the house opposite and puts a jug in front of Galileo's house.

6

1616: THE COLLEGIUM ROMANUM, RESEARCH INSTITUTE OF
THE VATICAN, CONFIRMS GALILEO'S DISCOVERIES

> The world of knowledge takes a crazy turn
> When teachers themselves are taught to learn
> Clavius sees the starry night
> And finds that Galileo's right

Hall of the Collegium in Rome.

It is night. Important Clerics, Monks, Scholars in groups. To one side Galileo alone. A boisterous mood prevails. Before the scene begins great laughter is heard.

A FAT PRELATE: Stupidity! Stupidity! Tell me one scientific theory they will *not* believe.

A SCHOLAR: That you have an unconquerable loathing for food, Monsignore?

FAT PRELATE: They'll swallow it! They'll swallow it! Only commonsense goes unbelieved today. That there's a Devil, they doubt. That the earth spins like a marble in the gutter, they believe.

A MONK, *playacting*: I'm going dizzy. The earth's whizzing round. Grab me, professor. *He pretends to be swaying and holds on to a Scholar.*

THE SCHOLAR, *playing along*: Old mother earth's pissed again. *He holds on to another.*

MONK: We're sliding off, stop!

A SECOND SCHOLAR: Venus is all over the place. I can only see half her bum. Help!

A bunch of monks forms who pretend, laughing, that they are trying to stop themselves being thrown off a ship in a storm.

A SECOND MONK: Don't get thrown off onto the moon, brothers! It's got horrible sharp mountains.

FIRST SCHOLAR: Dig your heels in!

FIRST MONK: Don't look down! I get vertigo!

A MONK: Vertigo in the Collegium Romanum? *Great laughter.* Impossible.

FAT PRELATE, *intentionally loud in the direction of Galileo*: Are you still investigating? It's a scandal!

FIRST ASTRONOMER, *angrily*: No we are not!

SECOND ASTRONOMER: I don't understand Clavius. If we're going to take every nonsense trumped up in the last fifty years as shining truth — where will it end? In the year 1572 a new star appears, far more brilliant than its neighbours, the fixed stars of the eighth and highest sphere. Before a year and a half is gone it fades and disappears back into oblivion. So must we ask — are the heavens not eternal and unchanging?

PHILOSOPHER: If we do not stop them, they will destroy all the stars in heaven.

FIRST ASTRONOMER: That is what we are coming to! Five years later the Dane, Tycho Brahe, calculates the path of a comet. It began above the moon and broke through every shell of every sphere — the very supports of heaven! It met with no resistance. No crystal refracted its light. So must we ask — where are the spheres?

PHILOSOPHER: It's monstrous! How can Christopher Clavius, the greatest astronomer of Italy and the Church, stoop to investigate such a thing?

FAT PRELATE: A scandal!

FIRST ASTRONOMER: But he is investigating it! He's sat in there, staring through that devil's tube!

SECOND ASTRONOMER: Principiis obsta! The rot set in when we began to calculate from the tables of Copernicus, a heretic — the length of the solar year, the dates of the eclipses of the sun and moon, the position of stars for years ahead.

A MONK: I ask you, which is better — to experience an eclipse of the moon three days later than the calander says, or to lose eternal salvation?

A VERY THIN MONK, *comes forward with an open Bible,*

thrusting his finger fanatically at a passage: What is writ in Holy Scripture? 'Sun, stand thou still upon Gibeon; and thou, moon, in the valley of Ajalon.' But how can the sun stand still if it does not move at all, as these heretics preach? Does Holy Scripture lie?

ASTRONOMER: No. And that's why we're leaving.

SECOND ASTRONOMER: Some phenomena are difficult for us astronomers — but must man know everything?

VERY THIN MONK: They make the home of the human race a wandering star. They pack men, animals, plants and the earth itself into a cart and drag it in a circle through an empty heaven. They make heaven and earth no longer exist. No earth, for it is a star in heaven. No heaven, for it is many earths. There is no longer any difference between above and below — between the eternal and the mortal. We know we die. Now they tell us heaven will die too. It is written — there are stars, sun, moon and the earth below. But that man says the earth is a star! There are only stars! We will live to see the day when these heretics say — there are no men and animals, there are only animals, man is an animal!

FIRST SCHOLAR, *to Galileo*: Signor Galilei. You dropped something.

GALILEO, *who during the above has pulled his stone from his pocket, played with it and finally dropped it on the floor and now bends down to pick it up*: Wrong, Monsignore. It fell up to me.

FAT PRELATE, *turns round*: Insolent prat.

Enter a very old Cardinal, supported by a monk. They make way for him respectfully.

VERY OLD CARDINAL: Are they still in there? Can't they slap this silliness down quickly? Clavius is meant to know his astronomy. I hear this Signor Galilei throws man out of the centre of the universe to somewhere on the edge. Clearly he is an enemy of the human race! Deal with him as such! Man is the crown of creation. Every child knows that. God's great miracle, his most beloved creature. How can there be people so perverse as to even give the time of day to these slaves of calculating tables? What man of God can countenance such idiocy?

FAT PRELATE: The gentleman is present.

VERY OLD CARDINAL: So. You are the creature. I no longer

see that well. But I do see a striking resemblance between you and that man — what was his name? — the man we burnt.

MONK: Your Eminence should not excite himself. Your doctor —

VERY OLD CARDINAL, *shakes him off*: You want to degrade the earth, though it gives you life and all you have. You foul your own nest! But I won't put up with it! *He pushes the monk away and begins to pace up and down proudly.* I am not any old creature, on any old star, circling around somewhere then gone with a puff. I walk on a solid earth, with a sure tread. It is still. It is the centre of the universe. The eye of the Creator rests on me alone. Around me sweep, attached to eight crystal spheres, the fixed stars and the mighty sun, created to pour light upon my world. And upon me — so that God can see me. Everything is irrefutably seen to depend on me, man, the work of God, the creature at the centre, the image of God, immortal and — *He collapses.*

MONK: Your Eminence has overstretched himself!

At this moment the door at the back opens and the great Clavius comes in at the head of his astronomers. He crosses the hall silently and swiftly without looking to either side and speaks, already at the exit, to a monk.

CLAVIUS: He is right.

He goes out, followed by the astronomers. The door at the back remains open. Dead silence. The very old Cardinal comes to.

VERY OLD CARDINAL: What is it? Have they decided?

Nobody dares to tell him.

MONK: Your Eminence must be taken home.

They help the old man out. All leave the hall bewildered. A little monk from Clavius's commission of investigation steps next to Galileo.

LITTLE MONK, *surreptitiously*: Signor Galilei, before he left Father Clavius said — now let's see if the theologians can put their rings back in the sky again! You've won. *He goes out.*

GALILEO, *tries to hold him back*: It has won! Not me, reason has won!

The little monk has already gone. In the doorway a tall priest appears, the Cardinal Inquisitor. An astronomer accompanies him. Galileo bows. Before he goes out, he whispers a question to a door keeper.

DOOR KEEPER, *whispering back*: His Eminence the Cardinal Inquisitor.

The astronomer conducts the Cardinal Inquisitor to the telescope.

7

BUT THE INQUISITION PUTS THE COPERNICAN TEACHINGS
ON THE INDEX (5TH MARCH 1616)

When Galileo was in Rome
He was a guest in a Cardinal's home
With wine, food and laughter the whole night through
Just one little thing they wanted him to do

Cardinal Bellarmin's House in Rome

A ball is in progress. In the vestibule, where two ecclesiastical secretaries are playing chess and making notes about the guests, Galileo is received with applause by a small group of masked ladies and gentlemen. He arrives accompanied by his daughter Virginia and her fiance Ludovico Marsili.

VIRGINIA: I'm only going to dance with you, Ludovico.

LUDOVICO: Your shoulder strap's loose.

GALILEO:
Do not fear, my daughter
A young man's look or laughter –
The eyes that catch a loosened lace
Will smile for you soon after
By candlelight in a darkened place.

VIRGINIA: Feel my heart.

GALILEO, *puts his hand on her heart*: It's fluttering.

VIRGINIA: I want to look beautiful.

GALILEO: Essential. Or they'll start saying the earth doesn't go round the sun after all.

LUDOVICO. But it doesn't. *Galileo laughs.* Rome talks only of you, Sir. From tonight, Rome will talk only of your daughter.

GALILEO: They say it's easy to look beautiful in the Roman spring. Even I look like a bloated Adonis. *To the secretaries*: I'm meant to wait for the Cardinal here. *To the couple*: Go and have fun.

Before they go into the hall at the rear, Virginia comes running back once more.

VIRGINIA: Father, the hairdresser in the Via del Trionfo took me first and made four ladies wait. He knew your name at once. *She goes out.*

GALILEO, *to the secretaries playing chess*: Why play the old style chess? Narrow, narrow. Today the big pieces move all over the board. The rook like that. *He demonstrates.* – the bishop like that – the Queen like that and that. Space, new problems, new strategies.

ONE SECRETARY: Not on our salaries. We can only afford moves like this. *He makes a small move.*

GALILEO: No no, my friend. Live grandly and the money will come for the grandest boots! Move with the times, gentlemen. Don't hug the coasts – take the plunge, out into the ocean!

The very old Cardinal from the previous scene crosses the stage, accompanied by his monk. He catches sight of Galileo, walks past him, then turns uncertainly and greets him. Galileo sits down. From the ballroom is heard the beginning of Lorenzo di Medici's famous poem on transitoriness, sung by boys.

'I who saw the roses die
And all their withered petals lie
On cold ground, know the truth:
Vain is the gaiety of youth.'

GALILEO: Rome. – Big party?

FIRST SECRETARY: The first carnival after the years of plague. All the great families of Italy are here tonight. The Orsinis, the Villanis, the Nuccolis, the Soldanis, the Canes, the Lecchis, the Estanis, the Colombis –

SECOND SECRETARY: Their Eminences, the Cardinals Bellarmin and Barberini.

Enter Cardinal Bellarmin and Cardinal Barberini. They are holding masks of a lamb and a dove on sticks in front of their faces.

BARBERINI, *pointing his index finger at Galileo*: 'The sun also riseth and the sun goeth down, and hasteneth to his place where

he arose.' So says Ecclesiastes the preacher. And what says
Galileo?

GALILEO: When I was so high *He indicates with his hand.* your
Eminence, I stood on a ship and shouted — the shore is
moving away. Today I know the shore stood still, and the boat
moved away.

BARBERINI: Neat. Neat. What one can see, Bellarmin, that the
stars revolve in heaven, need not be true. But what is true,
that the earth revolves, cannot be seen. Very neat. And his
moons of Jupiter are hard nuts for our astronomers to crack.
Unfortunately I too studied astronomy. It's an itch you can't
scratch away.

BELLARMIN: Move with the times, Barberini. If new star charts,
whatever theory they're based on, make navigation simpler —
let our sailors use the charts. We only dislike teachings that
contradict the Bible. *He waves a greeting to the ballroom.*

GALILEO: The Bible. 'He that withholdeth corn, the people
shall curse him.' Proverbs.

BARBERINI: 'Wise men lay up knowledge.' Proverbs.

GALILEO: 'Where no oxen are, the crib is clean; but much increase
is by the strength of the ox.'

BARBERINI: 'He that ruleth his spirit is better than he that
taketh a city.'

GALILEO: 'But a broken spirit drieth the house.' *A pause.* 'Doth
not the truth cry aloud?'

BARBERINI: 'Can one go on hot coals and his feet not be burned?'
Welcome to Rome, friend Galileo. You know the legend of her
origin? Two little boys had milk and shelter from a she-wolf.
Ever since, all children have had to pay for the she wolf's
milk. But she gives all kinds of pleasures in return — from
conversation with my brilliant friend Bellarmin, to the favours
of three or four ladies of international repute. Shall I parade
them for you?

*He leads Galileo to the rear to show him the ballroom. Galileo
follows reluctantly.*

BARBERINI: No? He wants the serious conversation. Good. My
dear Galilei, you are bent on making the universe simple. But
are you sure you are not merely trying to make it more
manageable? *He leads him to the front again.* You think in
elipses, circles, equal velocities, simple movements your brain

can cope with. But what if it pleased God to make his stars move like this? *With his finger he draws an extremely complicated orbit at irregular speeds in the air.* What of your calculations then?

GALILEO: Eminence, if God made the world like that — *He repeats Barberini's orbit.* — then he would have made our brains like that — *He repeats the same orbit.* So we would see such movements as wholly simple. I believe in reason.

BARBERINI: I hold reason to be inadequate. He is silent. He is too polite to say he holds *me* to be inadequate. *Laughs and goes back to the balustrade.*

GALILEO, *angrily*: I believe in reason!

BARBERINI, *to the secretaries*: Don't take this down. It's a scientific conversation between friends.

BELLARMIN: Just for one moment consider the time and trouble it cost the fathers of the Church, and so many after them, to bring a little order into this filthy world. Don't you find it filthy? Consider the brutality of the landlords in the Campagna who whip their half-naked peasants all over their estates — and the stupidity of those poor people, who kiss their tormentors' feet in thanks.

GALILEO: Disgusting! On my journey here I saw —

BELLARMIN: Yes, such suffering confounds us. And life is made of it. So we saddle the responsibility for this terrible world upon a higher being. We explain there is meaning, that suffering and humiliation are part of one, great plan. But it does not entirely reassure. And now you want to accuse this higher being of ignorance about the universe. Is that — wise?

GALILEO, *preparing to explain*: I am a faithful son of the church —

BARBERINI: He is incorrigible. In all innocence he wants to prove to God his divine incompetence in astronomy. Are you saying God didn't study astronomy carefully enough before he wrote the Bible? My dear chap.

BELLARMIN: Don't you think it a faint possibility that the Creator knows a little more than the thing he created?

GALILEO: But gentlemen, if man misinterprets the stars, maybe he misinterprets the Bible.

BELLARMIN: But the interpretation of the scripture is, in the end, a matter for the theologians of the Holy Church. Is it not?

Galileo is silent.

BELLARMIN: You see. You are silent. *He makes a sign to the secretaries.* Signor Galilei, the Holy Office decided tonight that the teachings of Copernicus, according to which the sun is the centre of the universe and motionless while the earth is not the centre of the universe and moves, are foolish, absurd and heretical to the faith. It is my official duty to warn you to abandon this belief. *To the first secretary:* Repeat that.

FIRST SECRETARY: His Eminence, Cardinal Bellarmin, to the above mentioned Galileo Galilei — The Holy Office decided tonight that the teachings of Copernicus, according to which the sun is the centre of the universe and motionless, while the earth is not the centre of the universe and moves, are foolish, absurd and heretical to the faith. It is my official duty to warn you to abandon this belief.

GALILEO: What does that mean?

From the ballroom is heard a further verse of the poem, sung by boys.

Seasons of beauty pass away
Pluck the rose: it is still May.

Barberini motions to Galileo to be silent as long as the song lasts. They listen.

GALILEO: But the facts? The Collegium Romanum confirmed my observations.

BELLARMIN: With deep satisfaction, which does you great honour.

GALILEO: But the moons of Jupiter, the phases of Venus —

BELLARMIN: The Holy Office reached its decision without considering these details.

GALILEO: But all further scientific research —

BELLARMIN: Is safe and sound. Protected by the Church's view that we cannot know, but we can research. *He again greets a guest in the ballroom.* You are free to expound even this teaching, but as a mathematical hypothesis — not a truth. Science is the legitimate and dearly loved daughter of the Church, Signor Galilei. And none of us think for one moment that you want to undermine the Church's authority.

GALILEO, *angrily*: Authority's own abuses undermine it!

BARBERINI: Do they? *He taps him on the shoulder, laughing loudly*. My dear Galilei, don't throw out the baby with the bathwater. We don't. We need you more than you need us.

BELLARMIN: I'm dying to introduce the greatest mathematician in Italy to the President of the Holy Office. He is one of your greatest admirers.

BARBERINI: And will turn into a lamb at once. You'd have
done well to come in disguise too. Perhaps the worthy
garb of a scholar of the traditional school? It's my mask
that gives me a little freedom tonight. Disguised like this you
might hear me murmur – if there were no God, we would have
to invent him. Good! We put our masks on again. Poor
Galileo's not got one.

They place Galileo between them and lead him into the ballroom.

FIRST SECRETARY: Get that last sentence?

SECOND SECRETARY: I'm on it now. *They write energetically.*
Did you get the bit where he says he believes in reason?

Enter the Cardinal Inquisitor.

INQUISITOR: Did the conversation take place?

FIRST SECRETARY, *mechanically*: First Signor Galilei arrived
with his daughter. She was engaged today to – *The Cardinal
Inquisitor waives this.* Signor Galilei then instructed us in the
new manner of playing chess, in which the pieces go all over
the board contrary to the rules of the game.

INQUISITOR, *waives this*: The transcript.

*A secretary hands him the transcript and the Inquisitor sits
down to run through it. Two young ladies in masks cross the
stage. They curtsey to the Inquisitor.*

ONE YOUNG LADY: Who is that?

THE OTHER: The Cardinal Inquisitor.

*They giggle and go out. Enter Virginia, looking round in search
of something.*

INQUISITOR, *from his corner*: Well, my daughter?

VIRGINIA, *is a little startled as she has not seen him*: Oh, your
Eminence!

*The Inquisitor extends his right hand to her, without looking up.
She approaches and, kneeling, kisses his ring.*

INQUISITOR: A superb night! Allow me to congratulate you on
your engagement. Your future husband comes from a noble
family. Will you remain with us in Rome?

VIRGINIA: Not at first, your Eminence. There is so much to do
before a wedding.

INQUISITOR: So, you will go back to Florence with your

father. I'm glad. I can imagine your father needs you. Mathematics is a cold companion, no? A fellow creature of flesh and blood nearby makes all the difference. A man can lose himself in the vast world of stars. Even a great man.

VIRGINIA: You are very kind, your Eminence. I don't understand these things.

INQUISITOR: No? No one eats fish in a fisherman's house, eh? Your father will be amused when he hears you finally learnt some astronomy from me, my dear. *Leafing through the manuscript.* I read here that our innovators, of whom your father is recognised the leader by the whole world, a great man – regard our present idea of the importance of our dear earth as somewhat exaggerated. Now. From the time of Ptolemy, a sage of antiquity, right up to today, the crystal spheres with the earth at their centre have been measured as some twenty-thousand diameters of our dear earth. A pretty space, but too small, far too small for our innovators. For them the distance of the earth from the sun – a vast distance, we always thought – is so infinitesimal, such a tiny nothing, compared to the distance of the earth from the stars of the highest sphere that they ignore it entirely in their calculations! Who can say our innovators do not live in a grand style!

Virginia laughs. The Cardinal Inquisitor laughs too.

INQUISITOR: Actually some gentlemen of the Holy Office are rather annoyed at such a view of the universe – which makes the cosmos of the Scriptures a mere bauble, of the kind one could hang around the neck of certain young ladies. They worry that in such enormous volumes of space a prelate and even a cardinal could get lost. Even God could lose the Pope. Yes it is funny. But I am happy, my child, that you will stay near your father, whom we all take so very seriously. I wonder, do I know your father confessor?

VIRGINIA: Father Christophorus of Saint Ursula.

INQUISITOR: Yes, I am glad you will be with your father. He will need you. You may not think so now, but he will. You are still so young, and so very much flesh and blood – and greatness is a burden to those to whom God has given it, not always easy to bear. Of course, no mortal is so great that he cannot be prayed for. But I keep you from your fun my dear, and I'll make your fiancé jealous. And your father, for telling you something about the stars he will think quite out of date.

Run along and dance. But do not forget to greet Father Christophorus for me.

Virginia hurries off after a low curtsey.

8

A CONVERSATION

Galileo, feeling grim
A young monk comes to visit him.
He can't say no to a son of the poor
Who wants to study nature's law
Galileo – he can't say no

In the Palace of the Florentine Ambassador in Rome.

Galileo is listening to the little monk who whispered the verdict of the papal astronomers to him after the session of the Collegium Romanum.

GALILEO: No no, go on. Talk. The way you're dressed gives you the right to say anything at all.

LITTLE MONK: I have studied mathematics, Signor Galilei.

GALILEO: That could come in handy – if it makes you admit now and then that two and two are four.

LITTLE MONK: Signor Galilei, I've not slept for three nights. How can I recognise the decree of the Holy Office and the moons I see around Jupiter? I decided to say Mass early this morning and come to see you.

GALILEO: To tell me the moons of Jupiter aren't there?

LITTLE MONK: No. But I have fathomed the wisdom of the decree. It teaches me there is a danger to mankind in unrestricted scientific research. I have decided to give up astronomy. It is my duty to try to explain the reasons why even an astronomer can abandon his work on the new theories.

GALILEO: I know the reasons only too well.

LITTLE MONK: I understand your bitterness. You think of the Church's great powers.

GALILEO: Just say instruments of torture.

LITTLE MONK: There are other reasons. Let me speak of myself. I grew up the son of peasants in the Campagna. Simple people. When I observe the phases of Venus I see my family. They sit with my sister by the hearth, eating cheese. I see the roof beams above them, black with the smoke of centuries. I see their work scarred hands, holding their spoons. Things go badly for them. But in their hardship there is a hidden kind of order. There are the routine cycles of everyday life, from scrubbing the floor, through the seasons in the olive grove, to paying taxes. Whatever the disasters, life is regular. My father's back is not bent suddenly, but a little more with each spring in the olive grove, just as the births that disfigure my mother's body more and more come at definite intervals. From what do they summon the strength to drag their baskets up the stony path, dripping with sweat, to bear children, even to eat? From the continuity, the sense of necessity, given to them by the sight of the soil, the trees turning green each year, by listening to the Bible texts in the little church each Sunday. They are told God watches them, searchingly, almost anxiously, that the whole theatre of the universe was built around them so that they, the actors, can play their parts well, great or small. What would my family say if I told them that they are really on a small lump of stone, spinning endlessly in empty space around another star, an insignificant star, one among many? How can their patience, their submission to misery, be necessary or good? How can the Holy Scriptures be good, explaining and justifying the patience, the hunger and the misery when they're found to be full of lies? No — I see their eyes fill with fear, I see them drop their spoons on the hearth, betrayed and cheated. I hear them say — so, no one watches us, eh? We must look after ourselves, even though we are ignorant, old and worn out, eh? Nobody has given us a part to play, there is only this miserable earthly life on a tiny star, around which nothing revolves? There is no meaning in our misery, hunger is just not-having-eaten, not a test of strength — hard work is just stooping and tugging, no virtue. So do you understand that I see true, maternal compassion in the Decree of the Holy Congregation, a great goodness of soul?

GALILEO: Goodness of soul! What you mean is nothing's left, the wine's been drunk, so let their cracked lips kiss the cassock! Why is nothing left? Why is order in this country the order of an empty larder, and the only necessity that of working yourself to death? Between bursting vineyards, at the edge of full wheatfields? Because your Campagna peasants pays for the wars the representative of gentle Jesus is waging in Spain and Germany. Why does he put the earth at the centre of the universe? So that Peter's chair can stand at the centre of the earth! That's what it's really about. You're right – it's not about the planets, it's about the peasants of the Campagna. And don't give me that crap about the beauty of traditions, golden with age. Do you know how the Margaritifera oyster produces its pearl? By becoming dangerously ill, enveloping an excruciating body, like a grain of sand, in a ball of slime. It nearly dies. To hell with the pearl – give me the healthy oyster. Virtues don't depend on misery, my friend. If your family were well off and happy, they'd have all the virtues being well off and happy brings. These virtues of exhausted men come from exhausted fields and I reject them. My new water pumps work more miracles than their ridiculous drudgery. 'Be fruitful and multiply' – for the fields are unfruitful and the wars kill your children. Do you want me to lie to your family?

LITTLE MONK, *in great irritation*: The highest principles compel us to silence – for the peace of mind of suffering humanity!

GALILEO: Do you want to see a Cellini clock? Cardinal Bellarmin's coachman delivered it this morning. A perk for not disturbing the peace of mind of suffering humanity. The authorities offer me wine, made sweet with the sweat of your parents' brows – which are, as we all know, created in God's image. If I were prepared to be silent, it would be from really base motives – good living, no persecution etc.

LITTLE MONK: Signor Galilei, I am a priest.

GALILEO: And a physicist. And you see that Venus has phases. Look out there. *He points out of the window.* See the little Priapus, by the spring next to the laurel? The god of gardens, birds and thieves – boorish, obscene, two thousand years old! He told fewer lies. Forget that, all right, I'm a son of the Church. But do you know Horace's eighth satire? I've been reading him again – for a sense of balance. *He reaches for a small book.* A little statue of Priapus was put up in the Esquiline Gardens. Horace makes it speak.

'A fig-tree log, a useless piece of wood
Was I, when the carpenter, uncertain
Whether to make a Priapus or a stool
Decided on the God –'

Do you think Horace would have let the stool be censored from the poem and a table put in its place? My sense of beauty is wounded if Venus has her phases censored from my view of the universe. We can't invent machines for pumping water up from the river if we're not allowed to look at the greatest machine before our eyes – the heavenly bodies. The sum of the angles of a triangle can't be changed on the whim of the Vatican. I can't calculate the paths of flying bodies to explain the rides of witches on their broomsticks as well.

LITTLE MONK: But won't the truth, if it is the truth, prevail – with us or without us?

GALILEO: No. No no. As much of the truth will prevail that we make prevail. The victory of reason can only be the victory of reasonable people. You talk of your Campagna peasants as if they were the mindless moss on their huts! How can you think the sum of the angles of a triangle will harm their interests! But if they don't wake up and learn to think, even the most beautiful irrigation system will be useless to them. For Godsake! I see the divine patience of your people, but where is their divine anger?

LITTLE MONK: They are tired out!

GALILEO, *throws him a bundle of manuscripts*: Are you or are you not a physicist? Here are the reasons why the tides ebb and flow. Censored! You're banned from reading it, right? Oh, you are reading it. So you are a physicist.

The little monk has become absorbed in the papers.

An apple from the tree of knowledge. He's cramming it in. He's eternally damned, but he's a glutton – he can't help it, he's got to stuff himself! Sometimes I think I'd let myself be locked up in a dungeon, ten fathoms underground, where no light could ever reach, if in return I could learn what it is – light. And the worst is – I must pass it on. Like a lover, like a drunk, like a traitor. It's a terrible vice. It'll lead to disaster. But how long am I going to stand shouting what I know up the chimney to no one?

LITTLE MONK, *points to a passage in the papers*: I don't understand this.

GALILEO: I'll explain it to you. I'll explain it to you.

9

AFTER EIGHT YEARS OF SILENCE GALILEO IS ENCOURAGED
BY THE SUCCESSION OF A NEW POPE, HIMSELF A SCIENTIST,
AND RESUMES RESEARCH IN THE FORBIDDEN FIELD. SUNSPOTS

> With truth in his pocket with tongue in his cheek
> Eight long years he did not speak
> But science could not wait temptation was too great
> Galileo challenged fate

Galileo's House in Florence

Galileo's pupils, Federzoni, the little monk, and Andrea Sarti, now a young man, are gathered for a practical lecture. Galileo stands reading a book. Virginia and Signora Sarti are sewing wedding clothes and linen.

VIRGINIA: It's fun sewing a trousseau. This is for a long table. Ludovico wants a lot of guests. But it's got to be very, very neat, his mother checks every stitch. She doesn't approve of father's books. Nor does Father Christophorus.

SARTI: He's not written a book for years.

VIRGINIA: That's because he realises he was wrong. In Rome a gentleman, high up in the Church, explained a lot about astronomy to me. The distances are too great.

ANDREA, *as he writes up the lesson for the day on the blackboard*: 'Thursday afternoon. Floating bodies.' Ice again — tub of water — scales — iron needle — Aristotle.

He fetches the objects. The others are reading books. Enter Filippo Mucius, a scholar of middle years. He seems somewhat disturbed.

MUCIUS: Can you tell Signor Galilei he's just got to see me? He condemns me without hearing me.

SARTI: But he doesn't want to see you.

MUCIUS: Please ask him. God will reward you. I must talk to him.

VIRGINIA, *goes to the stairs*: Father!

GALILEO: What is it?

VIRGINIA: Signor Mucius.

GALILEO, *stands up abruptly, goes to the stairs, his pupils behind him*: What do you want?

MUCIUS: Signor Galileo, I beg you, let me explain the passages in my book which seem to attack Copernicus. I —

GALILEO: Explain what? You agree with the decree of the Holy Congregation of 1616. That's your right. True, you studied mathematics with me, but that's no reason why I should expect to hear you say two and two are four. You are fully entitled to say that this stone — *He pulls a little stone out of his pocket and throws it down the hall.* — has just flown up into the roof.

MUCIUS, Galilei, I —

GALILEO: Don't talk to me about your problems! The plague didn't stop me.

MUCIUS: The plague is not the worst thing.

GALILEO: I tell you — he who does not know the truth, is only a fool. But he who knows the truth and calls it a lie is a criminal! Get out of my house!

MUCIUS, *tonelessly*: You are right. *He goes out.*

FEDERZONI: Very sad. But that's how it is. He's no great man. He'd be a nothing if he hadn't been taught by you. But now they say — he was taught by Galileo, he knows all his ideas — so he has to deny the lot, over and over again.

SARTI: I'm sorry for the gentleman.

VIRGINIA: Father liked him too much.

SARTI: I want to talk to you about your marriage, Virginia. You're still so young, you've no mother and your father only thinks of floating bits of ice on water. Not that I'd say ask your father about married life. He'd go barging round the house making dirty jokes for at least a week, and at mealtimes in front of the young people. No modesty. Never has had. I don't mean that anyway — simply what the future will be. Not that I'm wise, I'm an uneducated woman. But don't go blindly into a thing like marriage. What you want to do is go to a proper astronomer at the University and get your horoscope done. Then you'll know where you are. What's funny?

VIRGINIA: I've already been.

SARTI, *very eagerly*: What did he say?

VIRGINIA: Be careful for three months, the sun is in Capricorn. Then I'll get a favourable ascendant and the clouds will part. And if I keep Jupiter in sight, I can go on a long journey because I'm a Capricorn.

SARTI: And Ludovico?

VIRGINIA: He's a Leo. *After a short pause*. He's sensual.

A pause.

VIRGINIA: I know that step. It's the Rector, Signor Gaffone.

Enter Signor Gaffone, the Rector of the University.

GAFFONE: I've got a book Signor Galileo may like. For heaven's sake don't disturb him. A minute stolen from that great man is a minute stolen from Italy. I'll leave the book with you and slip away.

He leaves. Virginia gives the book to Federzoni.

GALILEO: What's it about?

FEDERZONI: I don't know. *Spells out*. 'De maculus in sole.'

ANDREA: Sunspots. Another one!

Federzoni hands it over to him irritably.

ANDREA: Listen to the dedication! 'To the greatest living authority on physics, Galileo Galilei.'

Galileo has buried himself in his book again.

ANDREA: I read the treatise by Fabrizius of Holland on sunspots. He believes they are swarms of stars passing between the earth and the sun.

LITTLE MONK: That's unlikely, isn't it Signor Galilei?

Galileo doesn't answer.

ANDREA: In Paris and Prague they believe they are vapours from the sun.

FEDERZONI: Mm.

ANDREA: Federzoni doubts that.

FEDERZONI: Don't drag me into it. I just said 'Mm.' I grind the lenses, you look through them — and what you see aren't spots, they're 'maculi.' How can I doubt anything? I tell you again and again — I can't read your books in latin.

*He gesticulates with the scales in anger. One pan falls on the floor.
Galileo goes over and silently picks it up.*

LITTLE MONK: There's happiness in doubt. I wonder why?

ANDREA: For two weeks on every sunny day I've climbed up
into the attic. A thin ray of light shines through a crack in the
shingles. You can catch the inverted image of the sun on a
sheet of paper. I have seen a spot, big as a fly, and blurred like
a little cloud. It moved. Why don't we investigate the spots,
Signor Galilei?

GALILEO: Because we're working on floating bodies.

ANDREA: Mother's got whole clothes baskets full of letters.
All Europe's clamouring for your opinion. Your reputation's
grown so great you can't keep silent.

GALILEO: Rome lets my reputation grow so great because I am
silent.

FEDERZONI: How can you bear to say nothing?

GALILEO: Because I can't bear being roasted on a woodfire
like a ham.

ANDREA: You think sunspots have something to do with that
other matter?

Galileo does not answer.

ANDREA: All right. Let's stick to bits of ice. They can't hurt
you.

GALILEO: Correct. Andrea — our thesis!

ANDREA: With floating, we assume it is not the shape of the
body that matters, but whether it is lighter or heavier than
water.

GALILEO: What does Aristotle say?

LITTLE MONK: 'Discus latus platique —'

GALILEO: Translate translate!

LITTLE MONK: 'A broad and flat disc is able to float on water,
whereas an iron needle sinks.'

GALILEO: Why does Aristotle say the ice doesn't sink?

LITTLE MONK: Because it is broad and flat and therefore
cannot divide the water.

GALILEO: Right. *He takes the piece of ice and puts it in the tub of water.* I press the ice down to the bottom of the tub. I remove the pressure of my hands. What happens?

LITTLE MONK: It rises up to the top again.

GALILEO: Correct. Apparently it can divide the water when it rises, Fulganzio!

LITTLE MONK: But why does it float at all then? Ice is heavier than water, because it is condensed water.

GALILEO: What if it were thinned water?

ANDREA: It must be lighter than water, otherwise it wouldn't float. Everything lighter than water floats — everything heavier, sinks. Which is what we have to prove.

GALILEO: Andrea, learn to think carefully. Give me the iron needle. Sheet of paper. Is iron heavier than water?

ANDREA: Yes.

Galileo lays the needle on a sheet of paper and floats it on the water. A pause.

GALILEO: What's happening?

FEDERZONI: The needle's floating! Holy Aristotle, no one checked up on him!

They laugh.

GALILEO: A great cause of the poverty of science is imaginary wealth. It is not the aim of science to open a door to infinite wisdom — but to put an end to infinite error. Write up your notes.

VIRGINIA: What's the matter?

SARTI: When they laugh like that my flesh crawls. I think — what are they laughing about now?

VIRGINIA: Father says theologians have their bell ringing, physicists have their laughter.

SARTI: I'm glad he doesn't look through the telescope so much. That was even worse.

VIRGINIA: Now he just puts bits of ice on water. No harm in that.

SARTI: I don't know.

Enter Ludovico Marsili in travelling clothes, followed by a servant carrying pieces of luggage. Virginia runs up to him and embraces him.

VIRGINIA: Why didn't you write and say you were coming?

LUDOVICO: I was near you, looking over our vineyards at Bucciole. I couldn't keep away.

GALILEO, *as if near sighted*: Who's that?

VIRGINIA: Ludovico.

LITTLE MONK: Can't you see him?

GALILEO: Oh yes. Ludovico. *Walks towards him*. How are the horses?

LUDOVICO: Doing very well, Sir.

GALILEO: Sarti, a celebration. Get a jug of that Sicilian wine, the old stuff!

Signora Sarti goes out with Andrea.

LUDOVICO, *to Virginia*: You look pale. Country life will do you good. Mother's expecting you in September.

VIRGINIA: Wait, I'll show you my wedding dress! *Runs out.*

GALILEO: Sit you down.

LUDOVICO: I hear over a thousand students pack your lectures at the University, Sir. What are you working on at the moment?

GALILEO: Oh, routine stuff. Did you come through Rome?

LUDOVICO: Yes. Oh – my mother congratulates you on your admirable tact about the sunspot orgies of the Dutch.

GALILEO, *dryly*: Many thanks.

Signora Sarti and Andrea bring wine and glasses. They cluster round the table.

LUDOVICO: Rome has its sensation to gossip over in February. Christopher Clavius has said he fears these sunspots will stir up the whole earth-round-the-sun circus again.

ANDREA: Never fear.

GALILEO: Any other news from the Holy City, apart from hopes of new sins on my part?

LUDOVICO: You know, of course, the Holy Father is dying?

LITTLE MONK: Oh.

GALILEO: Who is mentioned as his successor?

LUDOVICO: Barberini, mostly.

GALILEO: Barberini.

ANDREA: Signor Galilei knows Barberini.

LITTLE MONK: Barberini is a mathematician.

FEDERZONI: A scientist on the Holy Throne!

GALILEO: So now they need a man like Barberini who knows some mathematics! Times are changing. Federzoni, we may yet see the day when we don't have to look over our shoulders when we say — two and two are four. *To Ludovico.* I like this wine. What do you think of it?

LUDOVICO: It's good.

GALILEO: I know the vineyard. The slope is steep and stony, the grape almost blue. I love this wine.

LUDOVICO: Yes, Sir.

GALILEO: There are little shadows in it. And it's almost sweet, but only 'Almost.' — Andrea, clear this rubbish away, ice, tub, needle — I enjoy the pleasures of the flesh. I've no time for the withered, tight-arsed lot who call them weaknesses. I say — pleasure is an achivement.

LITTLE MONK: What are you going to do?

FEDERZONI: Start the earth-round-the-sun circus again.

ANDREA, *humming*:
The Bible says, the Bible knows
The doctors swear and prove —
The Pope he holds it by the nose
But the earth keeps on the move.

Andrea, Federzoni and the little monk hurry to the experimental table and clear it up.

ANDREA: Maybe we'll discover the sun revolves too. How'd you like that, Marsili?

LUDOVICO: Why the excitement?

SARTI: You're not goint to start that Devil's work all over again, Signor Galilei?

GALILEO: Now I know why your mother sent you. Barberini rising! Knowledge will be a passion, research a delight! Clavius is right, the sunspots do interest me. You like my wine, Ludovico?

LUDOVICO: I told you.

GALILEO: You really like it?

LUDOVICO, *stiffly*: I like your wine.

GALILEO: So. Not only do you take a man's wine and his daughter, you want to take his work away too? What has my astronomy to do with my daughter? The phases of Venus don't change her arse.

SARTI: Don't be crude. I'll get Virginia.

LUDOVICO, *holds her back*: Marriages in a family like mine have nothing to do with sex.

GALILEO: Did they stop you marrying my daughter, all these years? Why, was I on probation?

LUDOVICO: My wife will have to make a good impression, in the family pew of the village church.

GALILEO: You mean – your peasants will only pay their rents if your wife is holy?

LUDOVICO: In a way.

GALILEO: Andrea, Fulganzio, get the brass mirror and the screen! We'll throw the image of the sun onto the screen, to protect our eyes. Your technique, Andrea.

Andrea and the little monk fetch the mirror and screen.

LUDOVICO: You signed. In Rome. That you wouldn't meddle with the earth-round-the-sun business anymore.

GALILEO: Oh that! We had a reactionary Pope then!

SARTI: Had! His Holiness isn't even dead yet!

GALILEO: As good as! Put a grid of squares over the screen. We will be methodical. Then we'll answer all those letters, eh Andrea?

SARTI: Good as? Good as? Fifty times the man weighs his bit of ice. But when he hears a bit of news he likes – he blindly believes it!

The screen is set up.

LUDOVICO: If his Holiness dies, his successor may love science – but he won't be able to ignore the love for him of the most noble and powerful families in the land.

LITTLE MONK: God made the physical world, Ludovico – God made the human brain – God will allow physics.

SARTI: Galileo, now I'll tell *you* something. I saw my son fall
into sin for these 'Experiments' and 'Theories' and 'Observations' and I could do nothing. You set yourself up against the
powers that be. They've warned you once. Great Cardinals
coaxed and petted you like a sick horse. It worked for a bit.
But two months ago, just after the Annunciation, I caught
you at it again with these 'Observations.' Up in the attic!
I didn't say anything – but I did run and light a candle to
St. Joseph. It's beyond me. When I'm with you, you show
signs of commonsense and say you mustn't, it's too
dangerous – but two days of experiments and you're as bad
as ever. If I lose eternal salvation because I stick with a heretic,
that's my stupid fault. But you've no right to trample all over
your daughter's happiness with your great big feet!

GALILEO, *morosely*: Get the telescope!

LUDOVICO: Guiseppe – put my luggage back in the coach.

The servant goes out.

SARTI: She won't get over this. You tell her. I'll not.

LUDOVICO: You're going ahead with this. Signor Galilei. My
mother and I live for three quarters of the year on our estates
in the Campagna. We can tell you our peasants are not all
worried by your Treatise on the Moons of Jupiter. They're
too hard at work in the fields. But it could worry them if they
learnt that frivolous attacks on the Holy Truths of the Church
go unpunished. Don't forget they are deadbeats, living in a
brutish state, who muddle up everything. They really are
animals – you don't know the half of it. They hear a rumour
of a pear growing on an apple tree – and run away from their
work in the fields to chatter about it.

GALILEO, *interested*: Really?

LUDOVICO: Animals. When they come up to the house, moaning
about some trifle, Mother's forced to hold a dog whip under
their noses. That's all that will remind them of discipline and
order and decency. Oh you see flourishing fields of maize from
your travelling coach, you eat our olives, our cheese – but
you don't know the trouble, the supervision it takes, to produce
what you enjoy so casually.

GALILEO: I never eat olives casually. *Roughly*. You're holding
me up. *Calls out*. Have you got the screen?

ANDREA: Yes. Are you ready?

GALILEO: It's not only dogs you whip to keep cowed, eh Marsili?

LUDOVICO: You have a fine mind. It's a pity.

LITTLE MONK, *astonished*: That's a threat.

GALILEO: Yes. I might stir his peasants up so they start thinking new thoughts. And his servants and his stewards.

FEDERZONI: How? They don't read latin.

GALILEO: I could write in the language of the people. For the many — Latin is for the few. For the new ideas we need people who work with their hands. It's they who want to know the causes of things — not the rabble who see the bread on the table but don't care how it was baked. They thank God, not the baker. Bakers — they will understand that nothing moves which is not moved. Your sister at the olive press, Fulganzio, won't be shocked — she'll probably laugh — when she hears the sun is no golden coat of arms, but a lever — the sun moves the earth.

LUDOVICO: You will always be a slave of your passions. Apologise to Virginia for me. It's better I don't see her.

GALILEO: The dowry is yours, anytime.

LUDOVICO: Goodbye. *He goes.*

ANDREA: Remember us to all the Marsilis!

FEDERZONI: Who order the earth to be still so their castles don't come tumbling down!

ANDREA: And the Cencis and the Villanis!

FEDERZONI: The Cervillis!

ANDREA: The Lecchis!

FEDERZONI: The Pirleonis!

ANDREA: Who kiss the Pope's feet as long as he tramples down the people with them!

LITTLE MONK; *also at the apparatus*: The new Pope will be an enlightened man!

GALILEO: So. We begin our observation of the spots on the sun. They interest us. We do this at our own risk. We do not count too much on the protection of a new Pope.

ANDREA, *interrupting*: But blithely confident of blowing away the star clouds of Signor Fabrizius and the sun vapours of Prague and Paris, and of proving the rotation of the sun.

GALILEO: With some confidence of proving the rotation of the
sun. I do not hope to prove I have been right up to now —
but to find out if I have been. I say — abandon hope, all you
who enter into an observation. Perhaps they're vapours.
Perhaps they're spots. But before we say they are spots, let us
say they are fishes tails. We'll question everything, everything,
all over again. And we won't run at it in great big boots, we'll
go at a snail's pace. And what we find today, we'll strike from
the record tomorrow. And only when we find it once more
will we write it in. And when we find something we want to
find, we'll look at it with fierce suspicion. So — we will now
start our observation of the sun with the determination to
prove the earth STANDS STILL! And only when we fail, when
we're beaten and licking our wounds, shattered and depressed,
will we ask — were we right, does the earth go round the sun?
He winks. But if all possibilities but that one vanish into thin
air, then — no mercy to they who did not observe but still shout
their mouths off. Take the cloth off the telescope! Point it
at the sun!

*They silently begin the observation. When the flaming image of
the sun appears on the screen, Virginia comes running on in her
wedding dress.*

VIRGINIA: Father! You sent him away!

She faints. Andrea and the little monk rush to her.

10

IN THE FOLLOWING DECADE GALILEO'S TEACHINGS SPREAD
AMONG THE PEOPLE. PAMPHLETEERS AND BALLAD SINGERS
EVERYWHERE TAKE UP THE NEW IDEAS. FOR CARNIVAL TIME
IN 1632 MANY CITIES IN ITALY CHOOSE ASTRONOMY AS THE
THEME FOR THE GUILDS' PROCESSIONS

A Market Place

*A ballad singer and his wife, looking half starved, arrive at a market
place with a five-year-old girl and a baby. A crowd, some wearing
masks, are waiting for the carnival procession. Both carry bundles,
a drum and other props.*

BALLAD SINGER, *drumming*: Honoured citizens, ladies and
gentlemen! Before the great carnival procession of the Guilds!
And at enormous cost, time, effort and trouble — we bring
you the latest song from Florence, entitled 'The terrible
teachings and opinions of the Court Physicist Signor Galileo
Galilei, or A Dose Of The Future.'

He sings.

When the Almighty made his great creation
He told the sun to get it right
And circle round the earth for illumination
Like a little maiden with her lamp alight
It was his wish that each and every inferior
Would circle round its one and only superior

And things began to whirl around
The lesser round the greater
The first around the later
As in heaven, so down among us on the ground

And round the Pope the cardinals
And round the cardinals the bishops
And round the bishops the secretaries
And round the secretaries the magistrates
And round the magistrates the artisans
And round the artisans the house servants
And round the house servants the dogs, the chickens
and the beggars.

That my good people is the Great Order itself,
Orde Ordinum, as the theologians say, regula aeternis, the Rule
of Rules. But what happened then my good people?

Up stands Professor Galileo
(Chucks the Bible away, whips out his telescope
looks at the sky and says —)
You sun up there you stop!
For now we know Creatio Dei
Has gone and blown up pop.

That's not so bad you lot if you like a joke
The servants get ruder every day — oh disaster!
Life is so bitter it makes you want to choke
Who doesn't want to be his own fine Lord and Master?

(Spoken:) Honoured citizens, such teachings are right up the
creek, impossible and not on.

He sings.

> Young men and women bold as brass
> The dogs asleep and overfed
> The choirboy now won't go to mass
> The drunk apprentice will stay in bed
>
> No no good people God's Bible is no joke
> The rope must be thick to break our necks — oh disaster!
> Life is so bitter it makes you want to choke
> Who doesn't want to be his own fine Lord and Master?
>
> So, good people, look into the future as the clever Galileo
>   Galilei sees it
>
> The builder digs the rich man's plot
> And slaps down brick and stone
> But when he sees the house he's got
> He moves in on his own
>
> No no good people God's Bible is no joke
> The rope must be thick to break our necks — oh disaster!
> Life is so bitter it makes you want to choke
> Who doesn't want to be his own Lord and Master?

SINGER'S WIFE:

> I'm setting out to have some fun
> I've told my man get out by noon
> I think I'll find another sun
> To show the mountains on my moon

BALLAD SINGER:

> No Galileo no no no stop it all
> Break a mad dog's muzzle the dog will bite— disaster
> That's right life's hard it's not fun when duties call
> Who doesn't want to be his own fine Lord and Master?

CHORALE:

> You wretched of the earth in pain and woe
> Rise up throw off your chains find strength in your distress
> And learn from the good Doctor Galileo
> The ABC of earthly happiness
> It's thinking like a slave that makes for weakness
> Who doesn't want to be his own fine Lord and master?
> His own fine Lord and Master.

BALLAD SINGER: We give you — the fabulous discovery of
  Galileo Galilei — the earth circling round the sun!

He beats violently on the drum. The wife holds a crude representation of the sun and the child, holding a pumpkin above her head representing the earth, circles round the wife. The Ballad Singer points triumphantly at the child, as if she were making a dangerous death-defying leap, as she walks jerkily in time to single drum-beats. Then there are drum-beats from behind.

A DEEP VOICE, *shouts*: The procession!

Enter two men in rags, pulling a little cart. On a ridiculous throne sits 'The Grand Duke of Florence,' a figure in a pasteboard crown, dressed in sackcloth, who is peering through a telescope. Above the throne a sign – 'Looking out for trouble.' Then four masked men march in carrying a great canopy. They halt and hurl a dummy into the air representing a cardinal. A dwarf has stationed himself to the side with a sign 'The new age.' In the crowd a beggar raises himself on his crutches and stamps, dancing, on the ground, until he falls down with a crash. Enter a larger-than-life-size dummy, Galileo Galilei, which bows to the public. In front of it a child carries an enormous bible, open, with pages crossed out.

BALLAD SINGER: Galileo Galilei, the Bible smasher!

Great laughter from the crowd.

11

1633: THE INQUISITION SUMMONS THE WORLD FAMOUS
SCIENTIST TO ROME

> The depths are hot, the heights are chill
> The street is loud, the court is still.

Lobby and staircase of the Medici Palace in Florence.

Galileo and his daughter are waiting to be admitted to the Grand Duke.

VIRGINIA: It's taking a long time.

GALILEO: Yes.

VIRGINIA: There's that man, who followed us here.

She points to an individual who passes without taking any notice of them.

GALILEO, *whose eyes have suffered*: I don't know him.

VIRGINIA: I've seen him a lot recently. He scares me.

GALILEO: Nonsense. We are in Florence, not among Corsican bandits.

VIRGINIA: Here's Rector Gaffone.

GALILEO: Now he does scare me. He'll want to gossip for hours again.

Signor Gaffone, the Rector of the University, comes down the stairs. He is visibly alarmed when he sees Galileo and, convulsively turning his head away, walks past them stiffly.

GALILEO: What's up with him! My eyes are bad today. Did he even nod?

VIRGINIA: No. What did you write in your book? You don't think they say it's heretical?

GALILEO: You hang about in churches too much. All that running off to mass in the early morning makes you look pasty. You pray for me, don't you?

VIRGINIA: There's Signor Vanni the iron founder, you designed the smelting plant for. Don't forget to thank him for the quails.

A man comes down the stairs.

VANNI: Enjoy the quails, Signor Galilei?

GALILEO: The quails were superb, Signor Vanni. Many thanks.

VANNI: They're talking about you upstairs. They blame you for the pamphlets against the Bible that are selling everywhere.

GALILEO: I know nothing about pamphlets. My favourite reading's the Bible and Homer.

VANNI: Well, whatever's behind it — I'd like to take the opportunity of assuring you we manufacturers are on your side. I know nothing about stars — but you're a man fighting for the freedom to teach new things. Take that mechanical cultivator from Germany you told me about. Last year alone five books on agriculture were published in London. Here we'd be grateful for one book on the dutch canals. The same circles that harass you stop the doctors of Bologna cutting up corpses for research.

GALILEO: Your voice carries weight, Signor Vanni.

VANNI: Well I hope so. Do you know they have money markets in London and Amsterdam? And trade schools? Papers publish regularly, with the latest news. Here we've not even got the freedom to make money. They're against iron foundaries because they think too many workers in one place spreads immorality! I stand or fall with men like you, Signor Galilei. If they try anything against you, remember you have friends throughout the business world. The cities of Northern Italy are behind you.

GALILEO: No one's going to try anything against me.

VANNI: No?

GALILEO: No.

VANNI: As I see it, you'd be better off in Venice. Fewer priests. Take up the fight from there. I have a travelling coach and horses, Signor Galilei.

GALILEO: I can't see myself as a refugee. I need my comforts.

VANNI: Of course. But from what I heard up there, it's urgent. I get the impression they'd rather you weren't in Florence, just now.

GALILEO: Nonsense. The Grand Duke is my pupil. Besides, the Pope would slap a sharp NO on any attempt to trip me up.

VANNI: You don't seem able to distinguish your friends from your enemies, Signor Galilei.

GALILEO: I can distinguish power from impotence.

He walks away brusquely.

VANNI: Good luck to you, then. *He goes out.*

GALILEO, *comes back to Virginia*: Every Tom Dick and Harry
with a grouse latches on to me as a spokesman – and in places
where it does me no good. I've written a book about the
mechanics of the universe, that's all. What others make or
do not make of it is nothing to do with me.

VIRGINIA, *loudly*: If only people knew how you hated what
happened everywhere last carnival.

GALILEO: Yes. Give a hungry bear honey and he'll bite off your arm.

VIRGINIA, *softly:* Did the Grand Duke actually ask to see you today?

GALILEO: No, but I had myself announced. He wants my book.
After all, he paid for it. Ask that official. Complain we're
being kept waiting.

VIRGINIA, *goes to speak to an official, followed by the
individual*: Signor Mincio, has his Highness been told my father
wants to see him?

OFFICIAL: How do I know?

VIRGINIA: That's no answer.

OFFICIAL: No?

VIRGINIA: It's your job to be polite.

*The official half turns his back on her and yawns, looking at the
individual.*

VIRGINIA, *comes back*: He says the Grand Duke is busy.

GALILEO: You said something about 'polite'. What?

VIRGINIA: Nothing. I thanked him for his reply. You're wasting
your time here.

GALILEO: I begin to wonder if my time is worth anything to
anyone. Perhaps I'll take up Sagredo's invitation to go to Padua
for a few weeks, after all. My health's not too good.

VIRGINIA: You couldn't live without your books.

GALILEO: I could take a cask or two of the Sicilian wine along
with me in the coach.

VIRGINIA: You always said it won't travel. And the court owes
you three month's salary. They won't send it on to you.

GALILEO: That's true.

The Cardinal Inquisitor comes down the stairs.

VIRGINIA: The Cardinal Inquisitor.

In passing he bows low to Galileo.

Father, what's the Cardinal Inquisitor doing in Florence?

GALILEO: I don't know. He seemed courteous. I knew what I
was doing when I came to Florence and kept my mouth
shut for years. They praised me so lavishly now they've got to
accept me as I am.

OFFICIAL, *calls out*: His Highness, the Grand Duke!

*Cosimo di Medici comes down the stairs. Galileo goes up to him.
Cosimo stops, a little embarrassed.*

GALILEO: I want to show your Highness my Dialogues On The
Two World Systems —

COSIMO: Aha, aha. How are your eyes?

GALILEO: Not so good, your Highness. If your Highness permits,
I have the book —

COSIMO: Your eyes worry me. Really, they worry me. Perhaps
you have been using your wonderful telescope a little too
eagerly, eh?

He walks on without taking the book.

GALILEO: Didn't take the book, eh?

VIRGINIA: Father, I'm frightened.

GALILEO, *in a low voice and firmly*: Hide it. We won't go home.
We'll go to Volpi the glass-cutter. I have an arrangement with
him. A cart with empty wine casks always stands ready in the
tavern yard next to his shop to get me out of the city.

VIRGINIA: You knew —

GALILEO: Don't look round —

They are about to leave.

A HIGH OFFICIAL, *comes down the stairs*: Signor Galilei. It is
my duty to inform you that the Court of Florence is no longer
able to refuse the request of the Holy Inquisition to examine
you in Rome. The coach of the Holy Inquisition is waiting
for you, Signor Galilei.

12

THE POPE

A Room in the Vatican

Pope Urban VIII (formerly Cardinal Barberini) has received the Cardinal Inquisitor. During the audience he is being dressed. From outside the shuffling of many feet.

POPE, *very loudly*: No! No! No!

INQUISITOR: So. Doctors of all faculties, representatives of all the Holy orders and of the entire priesthood assemble with childlike faith in the Word of God as revealed in the scriptures, to hear that faith confirmed — and your Holiness will tell them the scriptures are no longer true?

POPE: I will not have the mathematical tables destroyed. No.

INQUISITOR: These people say it is the mathematical tables, not any spirit of rebellion or doubt. But it is not mathematical tables we have on our hands. A terrible unrest has come into the world. It is the unrest of their own minds they impose on the immovable earth. They cry — the figures compel us! But where do they get their figures? Everyone knows from where — from doubt. They doubt everything. Are we now to found human society on doubt, not faith? 'You are my master. But I doubt that is good.' 'That is your house and your wife. But I doubt that they should be yours and not mine.' So it spreads. Even your Holiness's love of art, which we have to thank for such beautiful collections, is slandered by slogans scrawled on the walls — 'What the barbarians left Rome, the Barberinis plundered.' And abroad? The Almighty will is pleased to beset the Holy See with many trials. Your Holiness's Spanish policy is misrepresented by ignorant men who regret the discord with the Emperor. Germany has been a slaughterhouse for fifteen years — they butcher each other spouting biblical texts. Plague, war and the Reformation have reduced Christianity to a few dwindling outposts. The rumour spreads through Europe that you are in secret alliance with Lutheran Sweden to weaken the catholic Emperor. And now these worms, these mathematicians, turn their telescopes to the skies and tell the world that your Holiness is even wrong about Heaven. One might ask why this sudden passion for the remote science of

astronomy? Who cares how the spheres revolve? But the whole
of Italy, down to stable lads, chatters about the phases of
Venus. And who does not think of all the other things,
declared absolute truth by the Holy Authorities, which are a
burden? What will happen if simple people, weak in the flesh
and prey to all kinds of excess, go over to believing in their
own reason? – which this madman declares the sole authority?
Once they doubt the sun stood still over Gibeon, they'll go on
to practice their filthy scepticism on the Gospels themselves!
They sail over the oceans. I've nothing against that – but they
put their faith in a brass ball called the compass, not in God.
Even as a young man this Galileo wrote about machines.
They think machines work miracles. But what miracles? They
don't need God, so what kind of miracles are they after? I'll
tell you – the miracle of destroying upper and lower, the
ruler over the ruled. Aristotle is a dead dog to them, but one
saying they quote everywhere – 'When the weaver's shuttle
weaves by itself and the zither plays by itself, the master will
need no apprentice and the ruler will need no servant.' They
think that's where they've got to now. That evil man knows
what he's doing when he writes his astronomical works in the
language of fishwives and merchants, not latin.

POPE: That is in bad taste. I'll mention it to him.

INQUISITOR: He whips up the one and bribes the other. The
ports of Northern Italy clamour for his star charts. We will
have to give in there. Commercial interests are at risk.

POPE: But the navigational charts are based on his heretical
beliefs. Star movements which cannot take place if we reject
his teachings. We can't throw away the teaching and keep the charts.

INQUISITOR: Why not? What else can we do?

POPE: Oh those shuffling feet. I can't stop listening to them.

INQUISITOR: They tell you more than I can, your Holiness.
Are the faithful to shuffle away from here, with doubt in their
hearts?

POPE: The man is the greatest physicist of the age! The light of
Italy! Not a common crank. And he has friends. Versailles,
the Court of Vienna. They'll call the Holy Church a cess pool,
stinking of prejudice. Get your hands off him!

INQUISITOR: One would not be forced to go very far with him.
I mean – practically. He is a man of the flesh. He'll give in at once.

POPE: He does celebrate his pleasures, more than any other man I've met. He even thinks from sensuality. He can't say no to an old wine or a new thought. I will not have physical facts condemned, I will not have slogans like 'The Church is the enemy of reason!' I allowed him to write his book if he ended with the opinion that faith, not reason, has the last word. He kept to that.

INQUISITOR: But how? In the book who argues for Aristotle? The fool. Who argues for Galileo? The wiseman. And which of them speaks the last word?

POPE: All right!

INQUISITOR: Not the wiseman.

POPE: All right! Yes. Yes that was impertinent. This shuffling in the corridors is intolerable! Is the whole world coming?

INQUISITOR: Not the whole world, just all that is good in it.

A pause. The Pope is now in full regalia.

POPE: The very most that may be done is to show him the instruments.

INQUISITOR: That will suffice, your Holiness. Signor Galilei knows all about instruments.

13

ON THE 22ND OF JUNE 1633, BEFORE THE INQUISITION, GALILEO GALILEI RECANTS HIS TEACHING ABOUT THE MOVEMENT OF THE EARTH

> There was a day in June when we were free
> And at the door a new age for you and me
> Oh what a day what went wrong
> A bright new age one day long

In the Palace of the Florentine Ambassador in Rome.

LITTLE MONK: The Pope won't see him. No more little chats about science.

FEDERZONI: He was the last hope. It's true what he said years

ago in Rome, when he was Cardinal Barberini — 'We need you.'
Well, now they've got him.

ANDREA: They'll kill him. The Discoursi will never be finished.

FEDERZONI, *looks at him furtively*: You think so?

ANDREA: Because he will never recant.

A pause.

LITTLE MONK: Stupid thoughts steal up on you, when you lie
awake at night. Last night I kept thinking — he should never
have left the Republic.

ANDREA: He couldn't write his book there.

FEDERZONI: And in Florence he couldn't publish it.

A pause.

LITTLE MONK: And I kept thinking — I wonder if they'll let
him keep the little stone he carries around in his pocket. His
proof stone.

FEDERZONI: You don't go with pockets, where they're taking him.

ANDREA, *shouting*: They won't do it! They won't dare! And if
they do, he won't recant! 'He who does not know the truth, is
only a fool. He who knows the truth and calls it a lie is a criminal.'

FEDERZONI: I don't think he will either. I'd not want to go on
living if he did. But they use force.

ANDREA: Not everything can be got by force.

FEDERZONI: Perhaps not.

LITTLE MONK, *softly*: He's been in prison for twenty-three
days. Yesterday was the great interrogation. Today is the
sitting. *As Andrea is listening, loudly.* Seventeen years ago I
came to see him there, two days after the decree. We sat there.
He showed me the little statue of Priapus in the garden. There,
by the sundial. He compared his work to a poem by Horace,
in which nothing can be changed. He said his sense of beauty
compelled him to seek the truth. He quoted a motto — hieme
et aestate, et prope et procul, usque dum vivam et ultra. He
meant the truth.

ANDREA, *to the little monk*: Tell him how he stood in the
Collegium Romanum, when they were examining the telescope.
Tell him!

The little monk shakes his head.

ANDREA: He behaved as usual. Stuck his hands on his behind, poked out his stomach and said 'I ask for reason, gentlemen!' *He imitates Galileo, laughing.*

A pause.

ANDREA, *about Virginia*: She's praying he'll recant.

FEDERZONI: Let her alone. She's almost lost her mind since they spoke to her. They've brought her father confessor from Florence.

The individual from the palace of the Grand Duke of Florence comes in.

INDIVIDUAL: Signor Galilei will be here soon. He will need a bed.

FEDERZONI: Has he been freed?

INDIVIDUAL: Signor Galilei is expected to recant at five o'clock before a session of the Inquisition. The great bell of St. Marks will be rung. The recantation will be read in public.

ANDREA: I don't believe it.

INDIVIDUAL: Because of the crowds in the streets, Signor Galilei will be brought back behind the Palace, to the garden door here. *He goes out.*

ANDREA, *suddenly shouting aloud*: The moon is an earth. It has no light of its own. Nor does Venus have light of its own and is like the earth and circles the sun. And four moons orbit the planet Jupiter which is in the region of the fixed stars and not attached to a crystal sphere. And the sun is the centre of the universe and motionless in space, and the earth is not the centre and NOT motionless. And he showed it to us.

LITTLE MONK: And force cannot make unseen what has been seen.

Silence.

FEDERZONI, *looks at the sundial in the garden*: Five o'clock.

Virginia prays louder.

ANDREA: I can't wait anymore! They're killing the truth!

He puts his hands over his ears, as does the little monk. But the bell is not rung. After a pause, filled by Virginia's murmured prayers, Federzoni shakes his head in the negative. The others let their hands drop.

FEDERZONI: Nothing. It's past five.

ANDREA: He resists.

LITTLE MONK: He will not recant.

FEDERZONI: No. How privileged we are!

They embrace. They are overjoyed.

ANDREA: So — force does not work, it cannot do everything! So — stupidity can be conquered, it is not invulnerable! So — man is not afraid of death!

FEDERZONI: The age of knowledge is born — now. Think if he had recanted!

LITTLE MONK: I didn't say so, but I was worried sick. I had no faith!

ANDREA: But I knew.

FEDERZONI: It would have been like night falling in the early morning.

ANDREA: Like the mountain saying — I am a sea.

LITTLE MONK, *kneels down, crying*: Lord, I thank you!

ANDREA: Everything is changed today. Tortured man lifts his head and says — I can live. So much is won when one man stands up and says NO!

At this moment the bell of St Marks begins to boom. All stand transfixed.

VIRGINIA, *stands up*: The bell of St Marks! He's not damned!

From the street below the crier is heard reading Galileo's recantation.

VOICE OF THE CRIER: 'I, Galileo Galilei, teacher of mathematics and physics in Florence, recant what I taught, that the sun is the centre of the universe and motionless, that the earth is not the centre and moves. I recant, curse and execrate with an honest heart and sincere faith all these errors and heresies as well as any other error or teaching contrary to the Holy Church.'

It grows dark. When it grows light again the bell is still booming but then it stops. Virginia has gone out. Galileo's pupils are still there.

FEDERZONI: He never paid you properly. You couldn't buy a pair of trousers, let alone publish anything yourself. You suffered all that because 'We were working for science.'

ANDREA, *loudly*: Unhappy the land that has no heroes!

Galileo has come in, completely transformed by the trial, almost beyond recognition. He has heard Andrea's phrase. For some moments he waits at the door for a greeting. When none comes, for his pupils shrink back from him, he walks slowly and unsteadily because of his eyesight to the front, where he finds a stool and sits down.

ANDREA: I can't look at him. Get him away from me.

FEDERZONI: Calm down.

ANDREA: Winebag! Snail eater! Have you saved your precious skin? *Sits down.* I feel ill.

GALILEO, *calmly*: Get him a glass of water.

The little monk fetches a glass of water from outside. The others do not pay any attention to Galileo, who sits on his stool. Far off the voice of the crier is heard again.

ANDREA: I can walk now, if you help me a little.

GALILEO: No. Unhappy the land that needs heroes.

Commentary in front of the curtain.

Is it not clear that a horse that falls from a height of three or four ells breaks its legs, while a dog is not hurt, nor is a cat from the height of eight or ten ells, nor a cricket from a spire, nor an ant if it fell from the moon? As small animals are proportionally stronger than the larger ones, so do small plants survive better: an oak two hundred ells could not support branches in the same scale as a small oak, and nature cannot allow a horse to grow as large as twenty horses or a giant to be the size of ten men, except by strengthening the body, particularly the bones, and distorting them out of all proportion. The common assumption that large and small machines are of equal strength is plainly false.

Galileo 'Discoursi'

14

1633 – 1642. GALILEO GALILEI LIVES IN A COUNTRY HOUSE
NEAR FLORENCE, A PRISONER OF THE INQUISITION UNTIL
HIS DEATH. THE DISCOURSI

> Sixteen hundred and thirty three
> To sixteen hundred and forty two
> Galileo Galilei was a prisoner of the Church
> Until the day he died.

A Large Room with a Leather Chair, Table and Globe.

*Galileo, now half-blind and old, is carefully experimenting with
a little wooden ball on a curved wooden rail. In the anteroom
sits a monk on guard. There is a knock at the door. The monk
opens it and a peasant comes in carrying two plucked geese.
Virginia comes out of the kitchen. She is now about 40 years old.*

PEASANT: I was told to deliver these.

VIRGINIA: Who are they from? I didn't order any geese.

PEASANT: I was told to say – 'From someone passing by.' *He
goes out.*

*Virginia looks at the geese in astonishment. The monk takes
them out of her hand and examines them suspiciously. Then he
gives them back to her, reassured, and she carries them by the
necks to Galileo in the large room.*

VIRGINIA: Someone passing by left a present.

GALILEO: What is it?

VIRGINIA: Can't you see?

GALILEO: No. *He goes over.* Geese. No name?

VIRGINIA: No.

GALILEO, *takes one out of her hand*: Heavy. Could do with a
bit of that right now.

VIRGINIA: You can't be hungry, you just had your supper. And
what's the matter with your eyes again? You couldn't see
them from the table.

GALILEO: You're in the shadow.

VIRGINIA: I'm not in the shadow.

She carries the geese out.

GALILEO: Cook them with thyme and apples.

VIRGINIA, *to the monk*: Send for the eye doctor. Father couldn't see the geese.

MONK: I need the permission of Monsignor Carpula to do that. Has he been writing on his own?

VIRGINIA: No. You know he dictates his book to me. You've got pages 131 and 132. They were the last.

MONK: He's an old fox.

VIRGINIA: He obeys the regulations. He's genuinely repentant. I watch him. *She gives him the geese.* Tell them in the kitchen to roast the livers with an apple and an onion. *She goes back into the large room.* And now we'll think of your eyes. We'll leave the ball alone and dictate a little more of our weekly letter to the Archbishop.

GALILEO: I'm not up to it. Read me some Horace.

VIRGINIA: Monsignor Carpula, to whom we owe so much — more fresh vegetables this week — told me every time he sees the Archbishop his Grace asks how you like the questions and Bible texts he sends you. *She has sat down to take dictation.*

GALILEO: Where was I?

VIRGINIA: Paragraph four: Concerning the attitude of Holy Church to the riots in the Grand Arsenal of Venice I agree with Cardinal Spoletti about the rebellious rope makers —

GALILEO: Ah. *Dictates.* I agree with Cardinal Spoletti about the rebellious ropemakers. It is better to dish out soup in the name of Christian brotherly love than to pay them more for their work. It is far wiser to strengthen their faith rather than their greed. The Apostle Paul says: Charity never faileth. How's that?

VIRGINIA: Very moving, father.

GALILEO: You don't think there's a whiff of irony?

VIRGINIA: No. The Archbishop will be delighted. He's very practical.

GALILEO: I rely on your judgement. Next?

VIRGINIA: A beautiful saying — 'If I am weak, then I am strong.'

GALILEO: No comment.

VIRGINIA: Why not.

GALILEO: Next.

VIRGINIA: 'And to know the love of Christ which passeth knowledge.' Epistle to Ephesians, iii, 19.

GALILEO: I thank your Grace for the marvellous quotation from the Epistle to the Ephesians. Stimulated by it, I discovered in our inimitable Imitatio the following. *Quotes from memory.* 'He to whom the Eternal Word speaketh, is relieved of much questioning.' May I take this opportunity of speaking of myself? I am still criticised for having once written a book on the heavenly bodies in the language of the market place. By doing so I did not intend to imply that books on much greater subjects, for example theology, should be written in the slang of pastry cooks. The argument for the latin liturgy — that through a Universal language all can hear Holy Mass in the same way — seems to me less happy. Our blasphemers are never at a loss for an argument and can object that in Latin no one understands anything. I gladly renounce the cheap intelligibility of sacred things. The latin of the pulpit protects the eternal truth of the Church from the curiosity of the ignorant — yet inspires confidence when spoken by the priestly sons of the peasantry in the twang of the local dialect. No cross that out.

VIRGINIA: All of it?

GALILEO: Everything after pastrycooks.

There is a knock at the door. Virginia goes into the anteroom. The monk opens the door. It is Andrea Sarti. He is now a middle aged man.

ANDREA: Good evening. I am leaving Italy to do scientific work in Holland. I was asked to look in on him on my way, to get news of him.

VIRGINIA: I don't know if he'll see you. You've not comeᵢbefore.

ANDREA: Ask him.

Galileo has recognised the voice. He sits motionless. Virginia goes into him.

GALILEO: Is it Andrea?

VIRGINIA: Yes. Shall I send him away?

GALILEO, *after a pause*: Send him in.

Virginia brings in Andrea.

VIRGINIA, *to the monk*: He's harmless. He was his pupil. So now he's his enemy.

GALILEO: Leave us alone, Virginia.

VIRGINIA: I want to hear what he has to say.

ANDREA, *coolly*: How are you?

GALILEO: Come closer. What are you up to? Tell me about your work. I hear — something to do with hydraulics?

ANDREA: Fabrizius in Amsterdam asked me to enquire after your health.

A pause.

GALILEO: I am well. They keep an eye on me.

ANDREA: I am glad I can report you are well.

GALILEO: Fabrizius will be pleased. Tell him I live comfortably. Through the depths of my repentance I manage to keep in favour with my superiors. They even let me study science. On a modest scale and under ecclesiastical supervision.

ANDREA: Yes. We heard the Church is pleased with you. Your complete submission has been effective. No doubt your superiors are happy that no new work with new ideas has been published since your capitulation.

GALILEO, *listening*: But sadly there are countries which still evade the Church. I fear the new teachings still thrive there.

ANDREA: No. Thanks to you a reaction has set in everywhere.

GALILEO: Really? *A pause.* Nothing from Paris, from Descartes?

ANDREA: When he heard of your recantation he threw his treatise on light in the drawer.

A long pause.

GALILEO: I am worried about scientific colleagues I led on the path of sin. Have they been enlightened by my recantation?

ANDREA: To do scientific work, I am going to Holland. One does not allow the bull to do what Jupiter will not.

GALILEO: I understand.

ANDREA: Federzoni is grinding lenses again in some shop in Milan.

GALILEO, *laughs*: Ah, no Latin!

A pause.

ANDREA: Fulganzio, our little monk, has given up research and returned to the bosom of the church.

GALILEO: Yes.

A pause.

GALILEO: My superiors look forward to MY spiritual
recuperation. I am making better progress than was expected.

ANDREA: Indeed.

VIRGINIA: The Lord be praised.

GALILEO, *gruffly*: Go and see to the geese, Virginia.

*Virginia goes out angrily. She is addressed by the monk as she
passes.*

MONK: I don't like that man.

VIRGINIA: He's harmless. You heard. *Going out.* We've got
fresh goat cheese.

The monk follows her out.

ANDREA: I'll travel through the night and cross the border in
the morning. Can I go?

GALILEO: Why come here Sarti? To upset me? I live cautiously,
I think cautiously. Even then, I have my relapses.

ANDREA: I don't want to upset you, Galilei.

GALILEI: Barberini called it the itch. Even he could not entirely
scratch it away. I've been writing again.

ANDREA: Oh?

GALILEO: I finished the Discorsi.

ANDREA: What? The 'Discourses, concerning two new branches
of knowledge: mechanics and the laws of falling bodies?' Here?

GALILEO: Oh, they give me quill and paper. They know deep
rooted vices can't be dug out overnight. They protect me from
nasty repercussions by locking it up, page by page.

ANDREA: Oh God!

GALILEO: Say what you want to say.

ANDREA: They make you plough water! They give you paper
and quill to pacify you. How can you bear to write at all?

GALILEO: I am a slave to my habits.

ANDREA: The 'Discorsi' in the hands of monks! And Amsterdam,
Prague, London hunger for them!

GALILEO: Yes, I can hear Fabrizius wailing for his pound of flesh, while he sits safe in Amsterdam.

ANDREA: Two new branches of science — lost!

GALILEO: No doubt it'll cheer him and others up to hear I've risked my few remaining comforts and made a copy. Sort of one hand behind my back. Sneaking out of bed the last six months, wringing the last drop of light from the brighter nights.

ANDREA: There is a copy —

GALILEO: My vanity's not let me destroy it yet.

ANDREA: Where is it?

GALILEO: 'If thine eye offend thee, pluck it out.' Whoever wrote that, knew more about comforts than I do. It's ludicrous folly to give it to you. But since I've not managed to keep away from science, you may as well have it. In the globe. If you fancy taking it to Holland, the responsibility's all on your head, of course. Say you got it off a clerk in the Holy Office with access to the original.

Andrea leafs through the manuscript.

ANDREA, *reads*: 'My aim is to establish a new science in an old subject, motion. I have discovered by experiment some of its properties which are worth knowing.'

GALILEO: Got to pass the time somehow.

ANDREA: This will found a new physics.

GALILEO: Stuff it under your coat.

ANDREA: And we thought you were a renegade! I was your bitterest critic!

GALILEO: And rightly. I taught you science and I denied the truth.

ANDREA: This changes everything. Everything.

GALILEO: Does it.

ANDREA: You hid the truth. From the enemy. Even in the field of ethics you were centuries ahead of us.

GALILEO: Explain that, Andrea.

ANDREA: With the man in the street we said — he will die but never recant. You came back — I recanted, but I will live. Your hands are tainted, we said. You say — better tainted than empty.

GALILEO: Better tainted than empty. Sounds realistic. Sounds like me. New science, new ethics.

ANDREA: I of all people should have known. I was eleven when you sold another man's telescope to the Senate of Venice. And I saw you make immortal use of it. Your friends shook their heads when you bowed and scraped to the child Duke in Florence – but you made science public property. Even then you were always laughing about heroes. 'People who suffer bore me' you said. 'Suffering comes from faulty calculations.' And 'When it comes to obstacles, the shortest line between two points may be the crooked one.'

GALILEO: I remember.

ANDREA: When you recanted in '33, I should have seen you were only getting out of a hopeless political brawl to carry on the real work of science.

GALILEO: Which is –

ANDREA: – the study of the properties of motion, mother of machines, which will shake the earth and demolish heaven.

GALILEO: Aha.

ANDREA: You gained the security to write the work only you could write. If you had ended in a halo of fire at the stake, they would have won.

GALILEO: They did win. And there is no scientific work only one man can write.

ANDREA: Why did you recant, then?

GALILEO: I was afraid of physical pain.

ANDREA: No!

GALILEO: They showed me the instruments.

ANDREA: There was no plan?

GALILEO: No.

A pause.

ANDREA, *loudly*: Science only knows one commandment – contribute to science.

GALILEO: And that I have done. Welcome to the gutter, brother in science, cousin in treachery! You eat fish? I've got fish. But it's not fish stinking, it's me. I'm selling out, you're a buyer. Oh dazzling sight of the book, the sacred goods! Mouths water, curses drown. The great Babylonian, the murderous cow, our holy, haggling, white washing death fearing society — opens her thighs and everything is forgiven!

ANDREA: Fear of death is human! Human weakness has nothing to do with science.

GALILEO: Wrong! My dear Sarti, despite my delapidated state I can give you a few tips about this science, to which you've given your life.

A short pause.

GALILEO, *academically, his hands folded over his stomach*: In my free hours, which are many, I've thought how the world of science, of which I no longer consider myself a part, will come to judge my case. Even a wool merchant, apart from buying cheap and selling dear, must worry about the trade's future. As I see it, to be a scientist needs particular courage. Science is knowledge, won through doubt. By giving knowledge of everything to everyone, it breeds sceptics. Now, princes, landowners and priests hide their machinations from the people by keeping them in a narcotic haze of superstition and old words. The misery of the many is as old as the hills and declared changeless as the hills from all the pulpits and University lecterns. Our new age of doubt delights the people. They tore the telescope from our hands and pointed it at their tormentors. Selfish and violent men, who greedily gobble the fruits of science, suddenly felt its cold eye turn on a thousand year old but artificial mystery — which could clearly be got rid of by getting rid of them. They drenched us with threats and bribes, irresistible to weak men. But can we deny ourselves to the crowd and still be scientists? The movements of the heavenly bodies are clearer — but the movements of rulers and tyrants still remain incalculable to the people. The fight over the measurability of the heavens has been won by doubt — but the fight of the roman house-wife for milk must be lost again and again, through faith. Science, Sarti, is concerned with both fights. A humanity stumbling in this haze of superstition and old words is too ignorant to develop its own powers — let alone develop the powers of nature your researches reveal. What are you working for! I believe the only aim of science is to relieve the toil of human existence. If scientists are scared off by dictators and content themselves with piling up knowledge for knowledge's sake, science will be crippled and your new machines will only mean new hardships. In time you may discover all there

is to discover — but your progress will only be progress away
from mankind. The gulf between you and the people will
become so great that one fine day you will cry out in
jubilation over a new achievement — and be greeted by a cry
of universal horror. As a scientist I had a unique opportunity.
In my time astronomy reached the street. For a moment, in
extraordinary circumstances, the courage of one man could
have detonated a great upheaval. If only I had resisted! If only
scientists had a hippocratic oath, like the doctors, vowing to
use their knowledge only for the welfare of mankind! But now,
all we have is a race of inventive dwarfs who can be hired for
anything. The irony is, Sarti, I see now I was never in any
real danger. For a few years I was as strong as the authorities.
And I handed my knowledge over to those in power, to use or
not, abuse or not, in their own interests.

Virginia has come in with a dish. She stops.

I have betrayed my profession. A man who does what I have
done cannot be tolerated in the ranks of science.

VIRGINIA: You have been received into the ranks of the
faithful. *She carries on and puts the dish on the table.*

GALILEO: I'm going to eat.

*Andrea holds out his hand to him. Galileo looks at the hand
without taking it.*

GALILEO: You're a teacher yourself now. Can you afford to take
a hand like mine? *He walks over to the table.* Someone passing
by sent me some geese. I still like eating.

ANDREA: So you no longer believe a new age has dawned?

GALILEO: Oh, a new age has dawned. Be careful when you go
through Germany, with the truth under your coat.

ANDREA, *unable to go*: About your criticism of the author we
discussed. I can't answer you. But I can't believe your
murderous analysis will be the last word.

GALILEO: Thank you, Signor. *He eats.*

VIRGINIA, *seeing Andrea out*: He doesn't like visitors from the
past. They upset him.

Andrea goes. Virginia comes back.

GALILEO: Have you got any idea who sent the geese?

VIRGINIA: Not Andrea.

GALILEO: Perhaps not. What's the night like?

VIRGINIA, *at the window*: Clear.

15

1637: GALILEO'S BOOK, THE 'DISCORSI', CROSSES
THE ITALIAN BORDER

Over the border in the night
The great book goes in secret flight
But we hope you'll keep in mind
You and I were left behind
Now keep the flame of science, the flame of science bright
Use it for mankind and use it right
Lest it makes a rain of fire to fall
Down upon us to consume us all

A Small Italian Border Town.

Early morning. Children are playing at the turnpike of the frontier. Andrea is waiting next to a coachman to have his papers examined. He is sitting on a little chest and reading Galileo's book. The travelling coach stands at the far side of the barrier.

CHILDREN; *they sing*:
    Mary Mary sat in a mess
    In her little pinky dress
    Got the dress all stuck with shit
    But in the snow and in the rain
    Mary wore the dress again
    Mary didn't mind a bit.

FRONTIER GUARD: Why are you leaving Italy?

ANDREA: I'm a scholar.

FRONTIER GUARD, *to the clerk*: Write under 'Reason for exit' — scholar. I must search your luggage. *He does so.*

FIRST BOY, *to Andrea*: Don't sit here. *He points at the hut in front of which Andrea is sitting.* A witch lives in there.

SECOND BOY: Old Marina is NOT a witch.

FIRST BOY: I'll break your arm.

THIRD BOY: She is a witch. She flies through the air.

FIRST BOY: Why won't they sell her even a jug of milk in the town, if she's not a witch?

SECOND BOY: How can she fly through the air. No one can do that. *To Andrea*: Can they?

FIRST BOY, *of the second*: That's Guiseppe. He doesn't go to school because he's got no proper trousers.

FRONTIER GUARD: What's that book?

ANDREA, *without looking up*: A book by the great philosopher Aristotle.

FRONTIER GUARD, *suspiciously*: What kind of bastard is he?

ANDREA: He's dead.

The boys walk around pretending to read mocking the reading Andrea.

FRONTIER GUARD, *to the clerk*: See if there's anything about religion in it.

CLERK, *leafing through it*: Can't find anything.

FRONTIER GUARD: No point in all this searching. No one'd hang under our noses what they've got to hide. *To Andrea.* You've got to sign we examined everything.

Andrea stands up hesitantly and goes into the house with the Frontier guards, still reading.

THIRD BOY, *to the clerk, pointing at the chest:* What's that? Look.

CLERK: Wasn't that there before?

THIRD BOY: The Devil put it there. It's the Devil's chest.

SECOND BOY: No. It belongs to the stranger.

THIRD BOY: Don't go in there. She's bewitched Passi the coachman's horses. I looked through the hole in the roof the snowstorm made and heard them coughing.

CLERK, *who has almost reached the chest, hesitates and goes back*: Devil's stuff, eh? Well, can't check everything. Where would that get us?

Andrea comes back with a jug of milk. He sits down on the chest again and continues to read.

FRONTIER GUARD, *following behind with papers*: Pack the luggage up again. Got everything?

CLERK: Everything.

SECOND BOY, *to Andrea*: You're a scholar. You tell us. Can anyone fly through the air?

ANDREA: Wait.

FRONTIER GUARD: You can go.

The luggage has been taken up by the coachman. Andrea picks up the chest and is about to go.

FRONTIER GUARD: Hang on! What's that chest?

ANDREA, *taking out his book again*: Books.

FIRST BOY: The witch magicked it.

FRONTIER GUARD: Rubbish. How can she bewitch a chest?

THIRD BOY: The Devil helped her!

FRONTIER GUARD, *laughs*: That won't work here. *To the clerk.* Open it.

The chest is opened.

FRONTIER GUARD, *reluctantly*: How many are there?

ANDREA: Thirty-four.

FRONTIER GUARD: How long will it take you?

CLERK, *rumaging superficially in the chest*: All printed. You can forget breakfast. And when do I get over to Passi to collect the tax on the sale of his house, if I've got to check thirty-four books?

FRONTIER GUARD: Yeah we've got to have the money. *He kicks the books.* Well, can't be much in that lot! *To the coachman.* Get on!

Andrea crosses the border with the coachman, who is carrying the chest. On the other side he puts Galileo's manuscript in his travelling bag.

THIRD BOY, *points at the jug which Andrea has left behind*: There!

FIRST BOY: And the chest has gone! See. It was the Devil.

ANDREA, *turning round*: No, it was me. Learn to look hard. The milk and the jug are paid for. Give it to the old woman. And I've not answered your question, Guiseppe. No you can't fly through the air on a stick. You'd have to have a machine on it. But there isn't such a machine. Perhaps there never will be, because man is too heavy. But we can't know that. We don't know nearly enough, Guiseppe. We're really only at the beginning.